SANIBEL ISLAND

Lynn Stone

VOYAGEUR PRESS

For my mother and father, who introduced me to Sanibel Island; for my wife, Lynda, who loves Sanibel's shops as keenly as its beaches; and for our daughter, Brittany, the little sandpiper who is showing us both the natural wonders of Sanibel through new eyes

Printed in Hong Kong through Bookbuilders Ltd.
91 92 93 94 95 5 4 3 2 1

Library of Congress Cataloging-in-Publication Data

Stone, Lynn M.
    Sanibel Island / Lynn Stone.
       p. cm.
    ISBN 0-89658-139-X
    1. Natural history—Florida—Sanibel Island. 2. Ecology—Florida—
Sanibel Island. I. Title.
QH105.F6S76 1990   90-44458
508.759' 48—dc20   CIP

Published by Voyageur Press, Inc.
P.O. Box 338
123 North Second Street
Stillwater, MN 55082 U.S.A.
In Minn 612-430-2210
Toll-free 800-888-9653

Voyageur Press books are also available at discounts for quantities for educational, fundraising, premium, or sales-promotion use. For details contact the marketing manager. Please write or call for our free catalog of natural history publications.

Above: The surf constantly gnaws on Captiva's gulf shore. Front cover: A white ibis dodges surf while hunting mole crabs. Back cover: In early evening, roseate spoonbills queue up to preen on a mud flat in the J.N. "Ding" Darling National Wildlife Refuge. Page one: Burrowing fiddler crabs honeycomb mangrove-clad shores. Fiddlers are named for the male's huge claw.

CONTENTS

ACKNOWLEDGMENTS

Taking the plunge, brown pelicans pitch toward the Gulf of Mexico off Sanibel Island for a late fish dinner.

Many people shared their time, hospitality, knowledge, and patience with me during the preparation of this book. My appreciation to Alice Anders, Sanibel conchologist; Karen Elling, rehabilitation specialist, CROW; Dr. John Flowers, photographer; Bill Hammond, director, Lee County Schools Environmental Education Program; Ed Hanley, Jr., charter boat captain; Suzy Johnson, manager, the Shell Net; Dr. James Layne, senior research biologist, Archbold Biological Station; Charles LeBuff, biological technician, "Ding" Darling National Wildlife Refuge, and director, Caretta Research; Doug Mackey, manager, "Ding" Darling National Wildlife Refuge; Ken Meeker, director, Sanibel-Captiva Chamber of Commerce; Kristie Seaman, education director, Sanibel-Captiva Conservation Foundation; John Solum, photographer; Mark "Bird" Westall, member, Sanibel City Council, and director, International Osprey Foundation.

4

INTRODUCTION

I am not usually excited by the sight of a toll-booth. Normally it provides me with about the same lift as a sand bur. The Sanibel causeway toll at Punta Rassa, Florida, is an exception, however. The toll is the last stop before the causeway and Sanibel Island.

The drive over the causeway to the island is exhilarating. It's just three miles across San Carlos Bay to Sanibel, but for me, that hop is a psychological leap. The view of blue-green San Carlos Bay and the edge of Sanibel looming ahead always stirs something within me. I have a camaraderie with this island. It has been that way since my first crossing in August, 1967.

Perhaps you have an Eden, a special place you once visited that stole part of your being and held onto it until you returned. Each time I get that roped and branded feeling, I try to recapture Sanibel's share of me.

The attraction Sanibel holds for me is, naturally, not the same appeal it has for everyone. I like the undeveloped half of the island where I can revel in mud, mangroves, shell-strewn beaches, and flurries of wings. My wife likes the undeveloped half, too; she's glad it's there—for me. In the solitude of a restaurant booth, she admits to a preference for Sanibel shops and eateries over black-necked stilts and estuaries, and then she asks, "What *is* a black-necked stilt?"

Fortunately, there are people who don't share our enthusiasm for Sanibel, otherwise the island would be overwhelmed. Natural selection takes over; some people just cannot adapt to Sanibel. It's too hot, too crowded, too humid, or too dull, they say.

A gentleman I'll describe, at the risk of being redundant, as a vocal New Yorker, held poolside court one afternoon in July. His greatest fear was that he would be forced to return to Sanibel. He was sprawled like a beluga on a deck chair almost within spitting distance of the Gulf of Mexico. He appeared quite comfortable, but I guess he missed the taxi horns and the intoxicating smell of the East River. Anyway, he grumbled that his wife was going to drag him back to Sanibel in November, "and," he added, "there's nothing to do at night!"

It is true. Sanibel night life is generally limited to beach walks and dining. In the context of New York and Miami, Sanibel's night life is zilch. Neon is a four-letter word here. The condos turn the beach lights down in the summer so that the sea turtles won't be frightened away. But the lack of lights and night life is a plus, unless you're intimidated by darkness and quiet. Or you're afraid of turtles.

Another, bigger plus is that civilization has tread carefully on Sanibel; it didn't trample. The geological and ecological artistry that shaped this island has been altered in the past six generations, sure. There are roads, homes, sidewalks, hotels, and some darn good restaurants and shops, according to my wife. Yet almost half of Sanibel remains undeveloped, unspoiled, raw as an oyster; and the other half has been developed with considerable forethought for the first half.

The purpose of this book is not to chronicle my life and times on the island or dwell on the partial decline of wilderness. Rather, it is to briefly introduce, consider, and most of all celebrate some of the many natural wonders that have survived on this unique island. May everyone who turns these pages find enjoyment in the natural beauty of Sanibel and help it to endure.

Least terns (Sterna albifrons), above, once nested alongside black skimmers (Rynchops nigra) on one of the Sanibel Causeway's spoil shores. The increasing popularity of windsurfing in the area prompted the birds to find new quarters on a spoil island nearby. The squatters' new digs are protected.

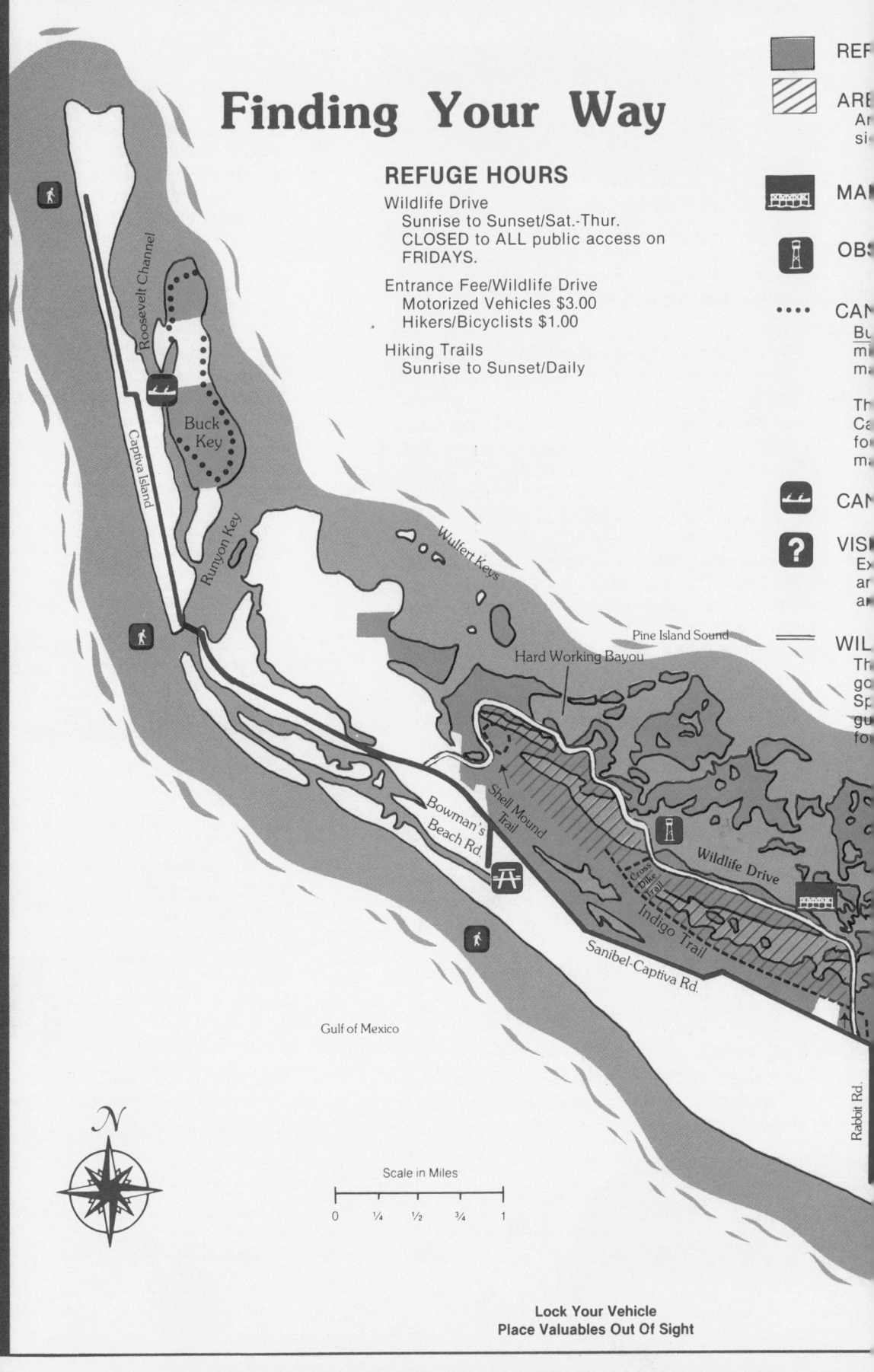

J.N. Ding Darling
NATIONAL WILDLIFE REFUGE

Finding Your Way

REFUGE HOURS

Wildlife Drive
    Sunrise to Sunset/Sat.-Thur.
    CLOSED to ALL public access on
    FRIDAYS.

Entrance Fee/Wildlife Drive
    Motorized Vehicles $3.00
    Hikers/Bicyclists $1.00

Hiking Trails
    Sunrise to Sunset/Daily

Roosevelt Channel

Captiva Island

Buck Key

Runyon Key

Wulfert Keys

Pine Island Sound

Hard Working Bayou

Shell Mound Trail

Bowman's Beach Rd.

Cross Dike Trail

Wildlife Drive

Indigo Trail

Sanibel-Captiva Rd.

Gulf of Mexico

Rabbit Rd.

REF

ARE
An
si

MA

OBS

CAN
Bu
mi
ma

Th
Ca
fo
ma

CAN

VIS
Ex
ar
a

WIL
Th
go
Sp
gu
fo

N

Scale in Miles

0   ¼   ½   ¾   1

Lock Your Vehicle
Place Valuables Out Of Sight

Blue-winged teal

Managing for Wildlife's Vanishing Habitat . . .

A number of wildlife management techniques are used on this Refuge to help offset expanding human development:

- **Water Management.** The dike, now used for the Wildlife Drive, was constructed in the 1960s as a mosquito control device. Today, in addition to controlling mosquito numbers, the dike benefits migratory waterfowl by allowing for water level manipulation.
- **Maintain and Preserve Habitat Diversity.** Exotic plants (not found naturally) have been planted on Sanibel for ornamental purposes. These plants now grow wild. They are crowding out native (naturally growing) plants that benefit wildlife by providing vegetative diversity. Exotic plant control is an important refuge wildlife management activity. Wilderness areas have been set aside to also help preserve naturally occurring wildlife habitat.
- **Law Enforcement.** Regulations are established to protect wildlife and their habitat. Enforcement and your compliance with these regulations are important. Refuge regulations are listed in the map legend.
- **Wildlife Research.** What does the endangered manatee require for survival? Finding the answers to this and other questions help ensure wildlife's survival.
- **Monitor Wildlife Populations.** Periodic censusing and duck banding are two methods managers use to monitor management results and wildlife health.
- **Public Information.** Your understanding and work towards wildlife's survival are very important. The Refuge's ability to communicate these needs to you is critical.

American alligator

Wildlife To Be Seen. . .

March through May, painted buntings, red-eyed vireos and other migrating songbirds may be seen. One of the most spectacular refuge scenes is that of the roseate spoonbills flying over the Drive near the observation tower at sunset. This often occurs during the spring at periods of low tide. Young yellow-crowned night herons, baby mottled ducks and immature little blue herons are out during the hot and humid summer season. Migrating songbirds such as the orange-crowned warblers, orioles and buntings again frequent the Refuge during the fall. December through February visitors can see blue-winged teal, red-breasted mergansers, white pelicans and other migrating birds.

Year-round residents include the often-seen osprey, the nocturnal raccoon, the large brown pelican, the gregarious moorhen and the alligator. Alligators can be observed basking in the sun, along the water's edge, to the left of the Drive. In the winter, they are seen during the sunnier parts of the day; but during the hotter parts of summer days, alligators seek cooler areas of the Refuge, where they are not likely to be seen. You are cautioned to stay on the trails and road to observe alligators.

The Refuge provides a place for approximately 291 species of birds, over 50 types of reptiles and amphibians and at least 32 different mammals. Because of this, you are likely to see a variety of animals during a journey through the Refuge.

The National Wildlife Refuge System. . .

J.N. "Ding" Darling National Wildlife Refuge is one of over 460 refuges in the National Wildlife Refuge System. The System, encompassing over 90 million acres, is a network of lands and waters managed specifically for wildlife. The Refuge System is administered by the U.S. Fish and Wildlife Service, an agency of the Department of the Interior.

This blue goose, designed by "Ding" Darling, has become a symbol of the Refuge System.

For More Information Contact . . .

Printing Courtesy Of

"DING" DARLING WILDLIFE SOCIETY
SANIBEL • FLORIDA

Refuge Manager
J.N. "Ding" Darling NWR
1 Wildlife Drive
Sanibel, FL 33957
813/472-1100

August, 1991

J.N. Ding Darling
NATIONAL WILDLIFE REFUGE

U.S. FISH & WILDLIFE SERVICE
DEPARTMENT OF THE INTERIOR

For An Enjoyable Visit. . .

Start your tour at the Refuge Visitor Center. The staff and volunteers will orient you to the Refuge. Take your binoculars and cameras, drive slowly, walk a trail and look closely. This will help you see animals that blend in well with their surroundings. Visit the Refuge during periods of low tide for the best wildlife observation opportunities. Tide changes occur on the Refuge one to two hours later than times stated on island tide charts. Sanibel was once known for its immense mosquito population. Currently, mosquito control practices keep insect population numbers down. Yet, you should be prepared for mosquitoes and other biting insects.

Jay Norwood Darling. . .

"Ding" Darling Refuge was named after one of the pioneers of the conservation movement. "Ding" is a shortened version Jay Norwood Darling used for his signature. This is how he signed his political cartoons, for which he received a Pulitzer Prize in 1923 and 1942.

Mr. Darling headed the U.S. Biological Survey (forerunner of the Fish and Wildlife Service) under Franklin Roosevelt's administration. He is also credited as one of the key people in the establishment of the National Wildlife Refuge System.

One of Mr. Darling's most important contributions to wildlife was the initiation, in 1934, of the Migratory Bird Hunting Stamp or "Duck Stamp" program. He designed the first stamp and every year since, a new stamp has been issued. The proceeds from the sale of these stamps have purchased wetlands for 200 National Wildlife Refuges. Duck Stamps are sold at the "Ding" Darling Refuge Visitor Center, for those who want to contribute to wetlands preservation.

In Times Gone By. . .

Sanibel is a subtropical barrier island composed of sand, shell and silt. Dry ridges and wet sloughs now exist on this 12-mile long island that is fringed with mangrove trees, shallow bays and white sandy beaches.

The Island was inhabited by Native Americans for over 2,000 years. Calusa Indians used the Island for a place to live and find food. During the mid-1800s, European explorers and settlers found and began to inhabit Sanibel. Farming and fishing provided a living for these settlers. In 1926, a hurricane destroyed the agricultural pursuits. Tourism has since become the economic foundation for residents of this Island that today is connected to the mainland by a three-mile causeway.

This 4,975 acre Refuge was established as Sanibel National Wildlife Refuge in 1945. It was originally a satellite of the former Everglades National Wildlife Refuge. The Everglades is now a part of the National Park System; this Refuge is today an independent station of the National Wildlife Refuge System. In 1967, the Sanibel National Wildlife Refuge was renamed the J.N. "Ding" Darling National Wildlife Refuge.

NDS

OSED
d line of area closed
ed to public access.

E OVERLOOK

ION TOWER

AILS
anoe trails provide 4
veling through a red
rest.

Commodore Creek
affords views of wildlife
d around the red
ee roots.

TAL LOCATIONS

NTER
audio-visual programs
free of charge. Hours

RIVE
ne-way drive enables
g of water birds.
is 15 mph. A self-
hure is available

----- **FOOT TRAILS**

The 1/3 mile Shell Mound Trail has
interpretive signs that inform
visitors about their surroundings.

Over 1¾ miles of trails are located
at the Bailey Tract, where alligators,
herons, egrets and other wildlife
are found.

The 2-mile long Indigo Trail
enables visitors to see ospreys,
wading birds and other wildlife.
The Trail starts at the Visitor
Center. Trail is closed at Cross
Dike on Friday.

FISHING (Note: FL State Fishing Reg. Apply)
Saltwater and freshwater fishing is
available along the Wildlife Drive, at
Tarpon Bay, and at the Bailey Tract.
No shelling allowed. Crabbing
permitted except in CLOSED
AREAS.

 **PUBLIC BEACH ACCESS**

SCCF **SANIBEL-CAPTIVA NATURE
CENTER**
This private center offers exhibits,
walking trails and guided tours.
Operating hours are posted.

PICNIC AREAS

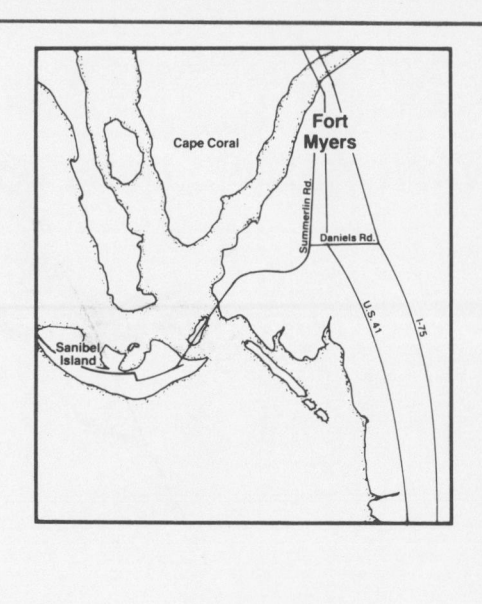

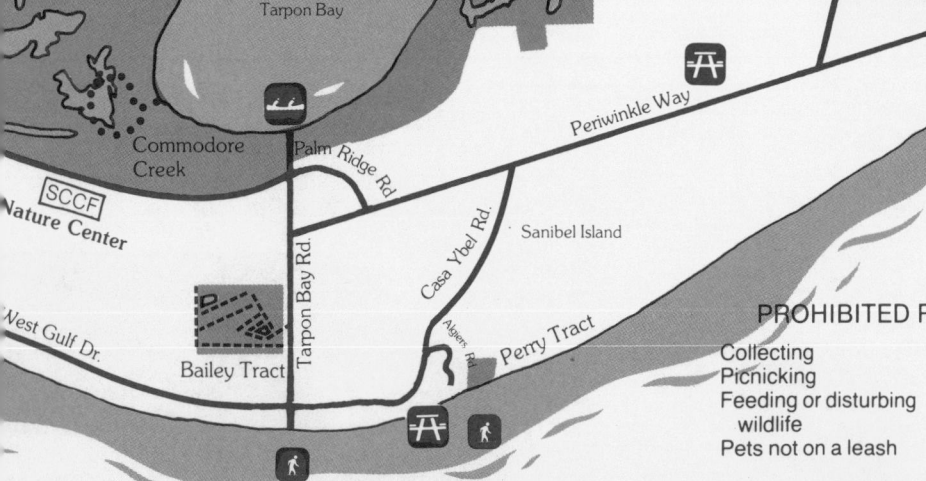

Mac Intyre Creek

Ladyfinger
Lakes

Shallow
Cut Off

Tarpon Bay

Causeway

Commodore
Creek

SCCF
Nature Center

Periwinkle Way

Palm Ridge Rd.

Casa Ybel Rd.

Sanibel Island

Tarpon Bay Rd.

Algiers Rd.

Perry Tract

West Gulf Dr.

Bailey Tract

PROHIBITED REFUGE ACTIVITIES

Collecting
Picnicking
Feeding or disturbing
  wildlife
Pets not on a leash

Camping
Boating on the left-hand
  side of the Drive
Crabbing with baited line or trap
Entry into Area Closed Zone

Possession of Firearms

BEYOND THE BRIDGE: SANIBEL

The causeway that strides from Punta Rassa on the Florida mainland to Sanibel Island is wonderfully unpretentious. Much of the three-mile causeway is spoil, the sand and marl dug from the bay bottom and knit with beach grasses. The road sections are stepping stones on the spoil to link the three humble bridge spans that rise gently over San Carlos Bay along the southwest gulf coast. They are not much higher, it seems, than the glistening backs of porpoises that roll beneath them.

The slivers of seashore along the road are favorite hangouts for beachcombers as well as for fish crows, gulls, pelicans, and knots of shorebirds. Black skimmers and least terns used to nest on a scrap of sand at the Sanibel end. The birds wisely moved to a spoil island in San Carlos Bay, and the little beach is now the launching site for flocks of windsurfers and their colorful rigs.

The causeway, then, does little to suggest the presence of the enchanted island on its seaward side. But the yellow road to Oz was paved with bricks, not gold, and Alice found Wonderland by tumbling into the depths of a rabbit hole. Sanibel, of course, is neither Oz nor Wonderland, and it does not have big, white rabbits. It is, however, a land of enchantment and amazingly singular qualities.

Sanibel is also, in geological fact, a barrier island, a mound of jungle-topped sand and shell rising—barely—from the Gulf of Mexico and facing the ocean's fury head-on. Barrier islands are numerous along the Florida coasts and elsewhere on the Atlantic seaboard, but Sanibel is a place apart. Much of its allure is obvious: twelve miles of tapered, white-sand beaches on the gulf side, a wealth of birds and seashells, and legendary weather with an average daily temperature of seventy-four degrees.

Sanibel is not a tropical island in the true sense. Still, at twenty-six degrees north latitude, it falls well into the temperate zone's southern range, so it is clearly influenced by the tropics. Its seasons, for instance, are delineated as much by the amount of rainfall as by changes in temperature and photoperiod. Like the tropics, Sanibel tends to have a summer wet season and a winter dry season. Much of Sanibel's plant life and some of its animal life—spoonbills, manatees, crocodiles—have tropical origins, too. The rare frosts that sneak down the Florida peninsula and onto the island serve as reminders of Sanibel's temperate zone roots. Fortunately for those fleeing northern climes, frost on Sanibel has the life expectancy of sea foam.

Sanibel is a uniquely accommodating island. No one feels compelled to do anything, yet there is plenty to do. The island is tailored to recreation, passive and active. Its woodland trails, still water coves, and beaches lend themselves to nature study, photography, endless wandering, and reverie. The island has tennis, golf, windsailing, boating, canoeing, fishing, swimming, biking, and, as the world knows, shelling. Traditionally,

7

From the mainland at Punta Rassa, the Sanibel Causeway strides across three miles of San Carlos Bay to Sanibel Island. Built in 1963, the controversial highway over the bay turned the tourist industry of Sanibel and sister island Captiva from a trickle into a torrent. One hundred and ten thousand vehicles passed over the bridge during 1964-65. Now some three million vehicles cross the bridge yearly.

Sanibel has been acclaimed for its world-class shelling. Sanibel's appeal today transcends shelling, which is just one of several attributes that draw increasing numbers of visitors and residents.

The island's greatest asset and the wellspring of its broad appeal is the fact that it is civilized wilderness, exactly what many of its patrons seek. Without the energy, compromise, and vision of its residents, the island could not have preserved so much of its natural beauty and character. At the same time, the island is blessed with, or cursed by, the conveniences of modern living. The proponents of total environmental integrity and the proponents of development have

struck a balance that is at the heart of Sanibel's popularity and distinction.

If Sanibel isn't pack-in, pack-out, bury-your-garbage wilderness, it isn't Miami Beach, either. For a broad spectrum of visitors, most of whom appreciate running water, Sanibel is a delightful blend of comfort and provocative wilderness. You can bathe in your own sweat on a morning canoe trip through a jungle of mangrove trees and swamp water, and fifteen minutes later be eating a lunch of fresh grouper or shrimp cooked and on a plate back in town. (If you use the running water first, figure another fifteen minutes.)

Many visitors to Sanibel like the small-town-within-a-resort atmosphere. For the most part

For the author's daughter Brittany, as for most children, the Sanibel beach is an endless trail of discovery. High on the list of finds are seashells—thousands of them. Shelling on the island isn't just for kids, however. Adult shellers tend to be more discriminating collectors than their offspring but no less enthusiastic.

rustic, tasteful, and unobtrusive, the shops and stores are largely operated by local merchants, most of them ex-patriate Yankees or Midwesterners with crusader zeal for the island. The churches, school, community theater, and other establishments are pleasantly small-town America. Meanwhile, back at the hotels and condos along the beaches, tourists gather, and the atmosphere is decidedly more cosmopolitan, especially during the busiest tourist season, mid-December through mid-April, when at peak times the combined population of Sanibel and Captiva, its sister island, exceeds fifteen-thousand.

Dining ranges from the informal fish sandwich in a weathered pub to a casually elegant dinner in one of the finer restaurants. It is much the same with accommodations, with choices ranging from beach cottages to full-service resorts.

Despite the development of parts of the island and a brush with ecological disaster in the 1970s, a fine bit of wild Sanibel and its wildlife persists. There is still abundance, from the hordes of fiddler crabs in pastel ceramic shells to clouds of shorebirds that sweep out over the sea as one. Perhaps that is the essence and the miracle of Sanibel—that so much is left of what was here in the first place, and that so far it has not been irreparably damaged.

Above: Like egret plumes, sea oats (Uniole paniculata) etched against a summer sunset near Sanibel's Gulfside City Park are studies in grace and form. Sea oats are protected by Florida law because their deep roots help stabilize sand and prevent erosion. Robust clumps of sea oats reach six feet in height. **Right:** The brown pelican (Pelecanus occidentalis) undergoes an amazing molt during its breeding season. The pelican's head becomes bright yellow and its neck molts from pure white to rich brown. Later, the yellow cap is replaced by white feathers. The brown pelican's vaunted gular pouch can hold about two gallons of water. The pouch is used to capture fish but not to store them.

Windsurfers launch their rigs from a shore along the Sanibel Causeway. On a breezy weekend, dozens of windsurfers raise their colorful sails and race across the sheltered waters of San Carlos Bay. Windsurfers share their corner of the sea with powerboats, fishermen, sea birds, and a multitude of aquatic creatures.

A squall blows out to sea after drenching Captiva Island one September evening. Afternoon and evening storms are commonplace during the traditional wet season in the subtropics of south Florida. The rains usually begin in June and last through September, offering almost daily respites from the heat.

LAND, WATER, AND WEATHER

Modern civilization didn't rush to Florida after Spain dealt the peninsula to the Monroe administration in 1821 or after statehood in 1845. It has been only in recent years, mostly since the wholesale use of air conditioning, that the state has faced an avalanche of development and tourism. Even today, first-time visitors to Florida are fond of noting that "everything looks so new!" By Florida standards, yesterday's newspaper is an antique. Anything built before the Kennedy Space Center is probably a national historic landmark. Sanibel's venerable lighthouse—its *historic* lighthouse—began operation in 1884. Some townspeople like to think that it predated *Tyrannosaurus rex*.

By the hands of geologic time, Florida itself is quite new. Sanibel Island is of even more recent vintage than the peninsula, probably having reached insular form only 5,000 years ago. It wasn't hurled up overnight from the sea in a volcanic frenzy, like Surtsey off Iceland's coast. Sanibel's genesis was far less spectacular. Ten thousand years ago, in a colder climate, Sanibel and its neighboring islands were part of mainland Florida. As the global climate gradually warmed, glaciers melted and the sea rose. Rivers and streams were flooded, and new bays and estuaries were created on what had once been firm ground.

When the sea rose, constricting the Florida peninsula, it left long, sandy coasts. Beyond these gently sloping shores lay miles of comparatively shallow sea. Waves rolling over ocean shoals break long before they crash against the main-land. When they break, they dredge up sand and shell and propel it in their path. Each wave helps build a ridge of accumulating sand and shell that runs roughly parallel to the beach. Over a period of hundreds or thousands of years, a ridge may become a barrier island. While its seaward approach confronts the ocean, its landward side typically borders a long lagoon or estuary. Scores of barrier islands, like Sanibel, Monomoy in Massachusetts, Hatteras in North Carolina, and Miami Beach were formed, more or less, in this way. Sanibel originally grew as a southeastward lobe of Captiva, according to geologist Thomas Missimer.

Sanibel is basically composed of sand and crushed shells, bound by layers of clay, mud, and vegetation. The ground doesn't shake each time the wind blows or the sea gets huffy, but the island does undergo constant geologic change, largely due to the energy of waves, currents, and storms. The level of the sea and the amount of sediment the ocean deposits and removes also contribute to the changing shape of Sanibel and all barrier islands.

Changes on barrier islands may be gradual, or they may be sudden and severe. Blind Pass, the saltwater inlet between Sanibel and Captiva, has been blocked and reopened many times over the years by storms. It was a storm, too, that slashed a passage—Redfish Pass—between Captiva and North Captiva islands in 1921. Undoubtedly another gale will someday plug the pass.

13

Added to the National Register of Historic Places in 1974, the Sanibel Lighthouse was constructed on Point Ybel in 1884, fifty-one years after Sanibel pioneers first petitioned the federal government for a light. Once dependent upon kerosene, today the light operates on electric power.

The clouds of a bright dawn are mirrored in the backwaters of Blind Pass, the restless finger of sea that separates Sanibel and Captiva. Gales periodically block and reopen the pass. The shores of Blind Pass are favorite gathering places of shellers and brown pelicans.

A more chronic form of change on barrier islands is natural erosion. This is a perfectly normal process, but the human residents of barrier islands find it most unnerving and expensive. Natural erosion has nibbled at Captiva's gulf shore for years. Residents and Lee County officials have fought the erosion at great expense, but without any permanent gains. The dynamics of barrier islands are such that the same forces of wind and water that built the islands will eventually change and reshape them. Geologists are quick to warn that these sea islands should not be treated as if they were permanent, immutable chunks of real estate. Storms, tides, currents, and the deposition of sediment are all natural phenomena in the evolution of barrier islands.

Sanibel enjoys the distinction of being the only barrier island on Florida's gulf coast with its long axis directed east and west. Sanibel is often de-scribed as being the shape of a shrimp. Its long, narrow tail is in the standard north-south axis, fronting the gulf. But the head of the shrimp bends eastward into San Carlos Bay. Like most barrier islands, Sanibel is long and narrow, no more than two miles across throughout most of its twelve-mile length. Just why Sanibel deviates from the orthodox north-south orientation is not clear. The reasons, however, are probably related to the interaction of currents and sediment from the sea and the Caloosahatchee River, which pours into San Carlos Bay northeast of Sanibel.

Sanibel has the topographical relief of a sand dollar. In fact, according to Sanibel historian Elinore M. Dormer, the island was once called *Puerto de S. Nivel*, or South Plane Harbor, on a Spanish map published in 1765. The name reflected Sanibel's low profile. The highest point in Florida is 345 feet above sea level. No one has looked for

Breaking waves dredge up sand and shells and propel them onto barrier islands such as Sanibel. Stacks of shells, the legacies of ebbing tides, often litter Sanibel's gulf beach.

Like other barrier islands, Sanibel's backside borders quiet, protected waters. At dawn, a reddish egret (Dichromanassa rufescens) chases minnows in a shallow bay framed by red mangrove trees (Rhizophora mangle). While many other members of the heron and egret tribe hunt with remarkable patience, the reddish egret, in contrast, typically hunts with rushes and quick jabs of its bill.

Noah's ark there. Yet barrier islands are even lower. The average elevation on Sanibel is four feet above sea level. It doesn't take Thomas Edison to figure out why Sanibel and its sister islands are easy prey for hurricane tides.

Despite its modest relief, Sanibel is not quite flat. Old beach ridges, the watermarks of relatively ancient tidelines, lie roughly parallel to the gulf shore. The significance of these ridges is that they form troughs for fresh water. Between one set of Sanibel ridges, which rise about four to seven feet above sea level, lie the island's major freshwater wetlands.

The freshwater wetlands consist of a loosely connected series of pools, depressions, and marshes. During the wet season they connect to form a single, sluggish drainage system some ten to fifty feet wide. Locally it's known as the Sanibel River, but it flows only during heavy rains and rarely exits to the gulf. The system is really an eight-mile-long slough. In 1960 the Army Corps of Engineers altered the Sanibel River somewhat by "channelizing" it—a process of dredging and straightening the river. The main purpose was to unify the little bodies of water so that mosquito-eating fish would have greater access to their favorite food.

In addition to surface freshwater, Sanibel Island has a freshwater aquifer. Rainfall that seeps through the ground collects in the aquifer, which acts as a subterranean reservoir.

During a normal year, about forty-two inches of rain pelt Sanibel, and 70 percent of Sanibel's rainfall occurs during the wet season. The wet season generally begins in June and winds down in October. On a typical summer day, thunderheads in the east begin stacking up in early afternoon. By late afternoon, the prevailing easterlies have driven thundering rain squalls over Sanibel. Sea oats buck in the wind and blinding rain spanks the island. After an hour or two the storm blows out to sea, rumbling toward the western horizon and later illuminating the night with bolts of electricity.

Periods of drought succeeded by hard, drenching summer rains are nature's way in the subtropics of south Florida. The plants and animals are adapted to that natural cycle. But the dry-and-wet cycle may be changing. Droughts seem to be more plentiful and protracted than at any other time in memory.

When summer rains fall, they offer a pleasant, cooling respite. Summers in southwest Florida are hot and humid. Even a dip in the gulf, where water temperatures climb into the eighties, isn't much more than an out-of-doors bath. Summer daytime temperatures on Sanibel range from the high eighties to the middle nineties. The sea and sea breezes moderate the heat, however, and the islands are more comfortable in mid-July than, say, Fort Myers, fifteen miles to the east.

Winter and early spring are the seasons of choice for snowbirds, the invaders who scramble to Florida when the snow flies in the northern states. Northerners favor winter and early spring because southwest Florida weather is usually warm and dry. Cold fronts that do slip down the peninsula from less hospitable parts of the planet depress temperatures into the forties or, rarely, into the numbing thirties and twenties, which scares the bejeebers out of the innkeepers.

When summer storm clouds glower over Captiva Island, the Gulf of Mexico stirs and the surf runs high on the island's sandy, gently sloping beach.

CALUSAS ON THE ISLANDS

By the time the Spanish explorers arrived in Florida early in the sixteenth century, the Calusa Indian culture had long been established in southwest Florida and on the islands of San Carlos Bay. The Calusas may have lived on Sanibel as many as 2,500 years ago. They almost certainly had become residents by 2,000 years ago. During their long period of occupation, they probably never reached a population greater than 200 on what is now Sanibel Island.

Although by the early 1800s the Calusas were virtually exterminated, their shell mounds throughout southwest Florida are testament to a once-flourishing culture, particularly in the Charlotte Harbor-San Carlos Bay region. Some of the mounds have been bulldozed or pillaged, but others remain intact, most of them overgrown with shrubs and gumbo limbo trees. The Calusas built their huts on the shell mounds, and the altitude of a mound gave them some protection during storm tides and perhaps some relief from the swarms of mosquitoes. They also used mounds for rituals and burial sites, as well as in constructing waterways and defense points.

Throughout most of their existence, the Calusas lived off the land. Excavations on Sanibel have turned up pots of clay, flint and whelk projectile points, shell implements, and tools crafted from deer antlers. Varieties of shellfish were a major source of food as well as construction material. The Calusas lived a simple existence; everything they needed was close at hand in the sea or woodlands. They were artistic, handsome, and fierce, hardly as undisciplined and primitive as the *conquistadores* may have expected.

The first European to have seen Sanibel may have been Juan Ponce de León in 1513. Some evidence, however, suggests that Amerigo Vespucci, an Italian in Spain's employ, may have explored southwest Florida in 1500. In any event, historians are quite sure that Ponce de León and his crew landed somewhere in Pine Island Sound or San Carlos Bay. Ponce de León hoped to find treasure, a spring of eternal youth, and native slaves. Ponce de León would have had more success taking sharks for slaves. The Calusas made it quite clear that they did not want to *habla el Español*. After several bloody skirmishes between the Spanish and Calusas during a three-week stay among the islands in the San Carlos Bay vicinity, Ponce de León pulled anchor and sailed south. Eight years later, in a second futile trip to the island region, Ponce de León was mortally wounded by a Calusa arrow.

Several years after Ponce de León's failure, Pedro Menéndez de Avilés anchored in San Carlos Bay. Menéndez de Avilés's mission was tuned more toward conversion than conquest, but Christian principles often clashed with native American culture. Menéndez de Avilés entrusted Jesuit Father Juan Rogel with the noble task of coordinating the conversion of the Calusas. Father Rogel observed that "wherever we Spaniards go, we are so proud and haughty that we crush all

Sanibel's original inhabitants, the Calusas, depended upon lightning whelks (Busycon contrarium) *and other marine mollusks for food, construction material, and projectile points.* Busycon *is still one of Sanibel's most abundant snails.*

The fertile sea and its shores helped provide the Calusas with natural bounty. The sea also provided them with uninvited visitors—the Spanish conquistadores. The beaches and birds, like the great blue heron (Ardea herodias) *survived. The Calusas were not as fortunate.*

before us." The Calusas, he wrote, were "untamed, restless, and evil beyond belief," but he added that his problems with the Calusas were small compared to the labor of keeping Spanish soldiers from hurting the Calusas.

This match was obviously not made in heaven. The Indians remained unimpressed by the warm glow of their saviours from Spain, whose forays into the New World gave new meaning to the phrase "Reach out and touch someone." The Calusas provided some warm glow of their own in 1569. Tired of Spanish high-handedness, they burned their own village on Mound Key and vanished into the woods. Without an Indian population to employ or proselytize, Menéndez, who had even bigger problems back at Spanish

St. Augustine, decided that the conversion was a lost cause. The Spanish pulled out, after which the Calusas returned to their haunts. Until the late 1600s, they prospered without undue Spanish interference.

The Calusas began to barter fish, hides, fruit, and other items with Cubans and, to a lesser extent, with Spanish traders in the 1600s. But as they began to dabble in commerce, they were assaulted by new and lethal enemies—tuberculosis, yellow fever, chicken pox, and measles—for which their strong will and arrows were no defense. By the end of the 1700s, the Calusas of Sanibel and the surrounding territory had become a vanishing people.

Gumbo limbo trees (Bursera simaruba) are rife on Sanibel and many other sea islands in southwest Florida. Easily recognized by their characteristic peeling bark, gumbo limbos flourish on the high ground of ancient Calusa middens. The gumbo limbo is representative of several West Indian trees that reach their northern range limits in south Florida.

When burgeoning development swept Sanibel in the early 1970s, some of the island's red mangroves were among the casualties. These shrubby, seafaring trees with cigar-shaped fruit spikes are essential to the welfare of coastal food chains. Mangrove detritus becomes the base of a complex food web along Florida's lower coasts.

AFTER THE CALUSAS

As the Calusas rapidly disappeared late in the eighteenth century from bouts with pestilence, slavers, and assorted human enemies, their influence dissipated. The islands of the southwest Florida coast became a refuge for runaway slaves, vagabonds, smugglers, traders, bands of Spanish Indians and Seminoles, and such migrant workers as pirates. If nothing else, the likes of many of these folks and their unbridled lawlessness helped give President James Monroe the excuse he needed to pry Florida loose from Spain in 1819. Seems that there were problems throughout Spanish Florida with American settlers running afoul of desperadoes. Monroe's message to Spain was essentially that if you can't protect Americans in Florida, give Florida to us and we will. The fact that Americans in Florida were in Spanish territory was apparently irrelevant.

Rumors of unsavory people and episodes among the islands of southwest Florida prompted the U.S. Navy in 1820 to send the schooner *Terrier* out of Key West to investigate. The *Terrier* reported nothing of consequence. Either the pirates, if there were any, had become choir boys, or they had had the good sense to take a cruise.

Unfortunately, the many stories about pirates in the Sanibel-Captiva region are based largely on heresay. Long John Silver's parrot probably would have been a more reliable witness than some of the humans who have expounded on piracy. No one really knows much about pirate activity here, and certainly the best tales cannot be proven.

One of the most familiar stories says that Captiva Island was the roost of the legendary José Gaspar, a.k.a. Gasparilla. The story further suggests that he kept his most lovely female captives on that island, hence the name, Captiva. The Gasparilla stories, according to historian Elinore Dormer, began with John Gomez, an old salt who lived on Panther Key. Gomez, who died in 1900, claimed to have sailed with Gasparilla.

If nothing else, Gomez' stories made good copy for Pat LeMoyne, public relations counsel for the Charlotte Harbor and Northern Railroad, a line that sang the disappearing railroad blues long before Arlo Guthrie. LeMoyne understood that the tales of piracy in the Charlotte Harbor area would be good for business at the stately Boca Grande Hotel. The hotel was at the end of the railroad on Gasparilla Island, just a few miles north of Sanibel and Captiva. One of the stories was that Gaspar's headquarters had been there on Gasparilla Island, and that he had beheaded a Mexican princess who spurned his attentions.

Despite slim pickings of factual data where pirates are concerned, Gasparilla's legend is secure in the islands. In 1984, David Silva, a Cheyenne, told Sanibel's *Island Reporter* that none other than Gasparilla had befriended the Calusas. A regular visitor to the islands, Silva was described in the article as an anthropologist specializing in the Calusas. At the time, Silva was beginning a journey to Captiva in a quest to find a lost cemetery. Silva said he was sure that Gaspar was a "real man" and that "the spirit of women is strong here." Gaspar, Silva told the *Reporter*, "didn't keep a lot of women here, but a few. They have to be buried somewhere. I hope it isn't under a condo."

* * *

The optimistic owners of the Florida Peninsula Land Company were a group of New York investors. They were ahead of their time, for in 1831 they purchased Sanibel Island as investment real estate. The land company bought Sanibel from an American bureaucrat, Richard S. Hackley, whose own title to the land was questionable. Nevertheless, the deal went through.

In 1833 a few hardy New Yorkers arrived to found the town of "Sanybel." The colony didn't prosper. The seventy or eighty colonists who were expected to arrive in the fall of 1833 to join the original band may or may not have reached Sanibel. But without a nearby mainland village to furnish supplies and act as a conduit for Sanibel produce, the settlement was doomed. By 1837 all of the colonists had deserted the island. Thoughts that anyone might have had about repopulating the island were discouraged by the outbreak of the Second Seminole War. When Florida became the nation's twenty-seventh state in March 1845, and when it skated from the Union in 1861, Sanibel was deserted.

In 1869 William Allen and his son George set up a castor bean plantation on one end of Sanibel. Castor oil was popular at the time, so it seemed like a good idea. When the 1870 census was taken, the Allens were the entire Sanibel population. They presumably abandoned Sanibel after a vicious hurricane raked the island in October 1873.

Interest in resettling Sanibel revived in the late 1870s. But by then the U.S. government had decided that it would build a lighthouse on the island and that the entire island would be a lighthouse reservation, a move that curtailed homesteading. Pressure to erect a light somewhere between the existing lights at Key West and Tampa Bay had been growing since the 1830s. Sure enough, on August 20, 1884, the long-awaited Sanibel light was activated, fueled by kerosene oil.

The Sanibel light stands today very much as it did in 1884. It sits atop a tall, steel cylinder braced by a latticework of wrought iron. Its open design helps insure that hurricane winds will pass through. Reaching upward 104 feet from Point Ybel on Sanibel's east end, the revolving beacon could be seen twenty miles at sea. The light operates now as an automated flasher in the care of the U.S. Coast Guard.

When the government backed off its homestead prohibition in the 1880s, settlers moved onto Sanibel and Buck Key, an island adjacent to Captiva and just a few steps from Sanibel's northwest shore. Not heavily wooded, Sanibel was attractive to farmers. For several years the little communities maintained farms of eggplant, peppers, tomatoes, watermelon, and grapefruit. In 1900, Clarence Chadwick established a coconut plantation on Captiva. The growth of Fort Myers, Henry Plant's steamship line, and the Atlantic Coast Line Railroad, which reached Fort Myers in 1904, made the export of island crops a profitable enterprise.

Had it not been for a hurricane, island farming might have continued unimpeded. A storm that Dormer called the "worst in island history" struck Sanibel in 1910. Fortunately, no one was killed, and the winds must have been worse than the tides, because Sanibel's farm economy continued to send food to market. In 1921 another hurricane assaulted the island and prompted a permanent exodus of many islanders. But the kayo to market farms was dealt by a hurricane on September 18, 1926. The sea plowed a fourteen-foot tide at the islands, covering virtually the entire surface with saltwater. The storm's brine was worse than its bite. The saltwater not only ruined crops, it drastically increased soil salinity, making planting futile until the salt leached out, which would not happen quickly. Suddenly and decisively the islands' future lay in their sunshine, sand, and shells rather than in their farming soil.

In 1928, the Kinzie brothers began operating a regular ferry service from Punta Rassa to Sanibel. The islands were still inconvenient to reach, but they didn't bask entirely unnoticed. Word leaked out. There were shells—mountains of them, some

A landmark in the town of Boca Grande on Gasparilla, the Gasparilla Inn was built in 1912. A nearby hostel of similar vintage, the Boca Grande Hotel, was torn down in the 1960s. The Gasparilla Inn, flanked by manicured lawns and palms, prospers long after the demise of passenger trains that once whisked tourists to Gasparilla Island for "the season."

said—and quaint, yet comely, lodges and remarkable views of a setting sun from silver beaches. The wealthy and the curious alike came to Sanibel and Captiva. The tourism began as a trickle, then gathered itself up, like the clouds of summer, in a storm the likes of which the islanders could never have imagined.

* * *

In the 1950s, with the rise of postwar interest in Florida, Sanibel became an increasingly popular destination. Lured by the promise of beaches littered with shells and the mystique of an island that could be reached only by ferry, the visitors massed on Punta Rassa. Business boomed for the car ferries, and high-season traffic waiting to board the ferry often backed up a mile. In 1958 the ferries hauled an average of 257 cars each day. The Kinzies thought about expanding the ferry

service, but they wisely resisted. Already they were seeing as many bridge proposals as cars.

The residents of Sanibel and Captiva, according to longtime Sanibel resident Charles LeBuff, were overwhelmingly opposed to a bridge to the mainland. The Lee County Commission, Sanibel's legal and political guardian at the time, nevertheless built the bridge after a series of legal battles involving a coalition of residents, the Army Corps of Engineers, the U.S. Fish and Wildlife Service, the Florida State Cabinet in Tallahassee, and the commission. At a cost of nearly $5 million, the bridge was completed in 1963.

Opening the bridge in 1963 changed the way of life on Sanibel and Captiva forever. At the same time, the bridge permitted access for many to an island world that had been the keep of a very few. Sanibel was hardly the last frontier, but the bridge bared it to an unparalleled and unexpected glut of tourists and developers. The island's accessibility

South Seas Plantation occupies over three hundred acres at the northern tip of Captiva Island. Clarence Chadwick once raised coconuts on what is now South Seas property, and coconut palms still garnish this seaside resort, which boasts eighteen pools, restaurants, a golf course, and a harbor and yacht basin.

The Island Historical Museum displays artifacts from the Sanibel and Captiva past in an appropriate setting—one of the oldest structures on the islands. Built in 1913, the museum is the former home of Sanibel pioneer Clarence Rutland, who died in 1982. The home was restored and moved to its present location on Dunlap Road, Sanibel, soon after Rutland's death.

made it fair game for everyone, and not everyone shared the same vision of the island's future. Battle lines were about to be drawn in the sand again.

In the decade after the bridge opened, Sanibel was lashed by a whirlwind of development. Artificial lakes were dug at the expense of natural wetlands. Along the gulf, condominiums sprang up on the dunes. Beach vegetation, vital in containing erosion and anchoring the dunes in storms, was routinely destroyed, and the buildings crowding the gulf became unnecessarily fat targets for hurricanes. On the bay side, mangroves were ground up with no regard for their crucial role in the life cycles of marine organisms. What might have been done with painstaking forethought for the Sanibel environment was instead being done helter skelter. Many residents watched with alarm as construction increased 72 percent between 1972 and 1973. Their restiveness turned to revolution when the county passed

zoning ordinances in 1973 that would have permitted housing on Sanibel for 90,000.

Having failed to prevail in its opposition to Lee County's recklessness, the Sanibel Planning Board boldly played its ace: home rule. In 1974 the voters passed a referendum to incorporate. The level of taxes would rise, but so would the level of expertise in protecting the island.

The planning board's argument for incorporation was that the island needed a comprehensive land-use plan to protect its future. When the new city government took over, it immediately stopped issuing building permits and began work on a plan. The plan was completed in July 1976 and provided for the long-term protection of natural resources and a reasonable amount of growth. It drew the admiring attention of enlightened cities in other parts of the country. And like the hurricane of 1926 and the bridge of 1963, it marked a turning point in Sanibel history.

Left: Beach morning glories (Ipomoea pes-caprae) *persist wherever dune vegetation has been protected on Sanibel. The plants lend more than color to Sanibel's high beaches: They help anchor the sand. After careless development in the early 1970s, Sanibel planners have been increasingly mindful of the island's fragile dune vegetation.* **Below:** *After the devastating hurricane of September 18, 1926, Sanibel's fortunes no longer lay in the island's planting soil. The future of the island's economy would lie in its sand, sunshine, and shells. Its reputation for shelling, in fact, became international. (Shown here: coquinas,* Donax variabilis.)

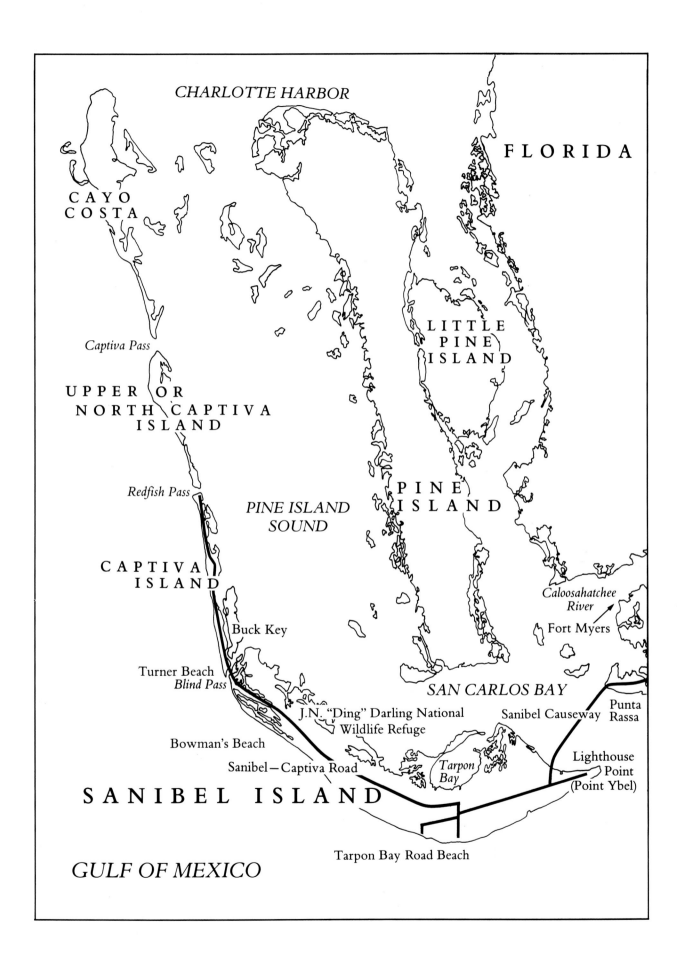

The black-bellied plover (Pluvialis squatarola) in breeding plumage is a dandy among Sanibel shorebirds. This bird, photographed in May, will soon be en route to nesting grounds near the Arctic Circle. On its return flight to Sanibel in September, the plover will be drab gray and brown.

BEACH AND DUNE

The gulf-front beaches of Sanibel and Captiva are spellbinding, their shifts in mood an opiate for everyone who steps upon them. The beach may be dazzling in sunshine one day and melancholy under a sheaf of clouds the next. At dawn and dusk, it is beguiling.

The dawn beach wakes in gentle light. Shell hunters, joggers, and quick-stepping plovers love the beach at dawn. The evening shore is no less inviting; watching the sun melt into the gulf is a favorite pastime on the islands. And it is no wonder. The wet sand of the wash may be streaked with the red of old lanterns, and if you stand on the rain-splattered beach and watch the sun set beneath the just-passed fury of a thunderstorm, the seashore is lit in radiant misty gold.

Seasons bring change to the shore, too. Winters are mild, but there are brisk days when the wind snaps at browning sea oats, and fine particles of sand pinwheel from the beach to the dunes. These are rock and roll days for ducks and loons that rise on swells and disappear in troughs. These are straight-up, cider-cool days for beachcombers. Sea foam skips onto the beach. Teased by the wind, it sideslips into the wrack, a jumbled ribbon of shells, seaweed, jellyfish, crabs, and other discards of an angry sea. Shorebirds colored like the sand huddle on the beach.

The Sanibel-Captiva beaches are worlds of changing light, mood, season, tide, and even dimension. The beaches are also worlds of ecological zones and niches, each with plants and animals adapted to its special conditions. The surf zone is the rendezvous of land and sea, a turbulent, intertidal community whose perimeters change with each tide. The marine animals of the surf zone may go almost unobserved. They are largely burrowers, and their tunneling saves them from being thrown ashore or swept to sea. Mole crabs, also known as sand fleas, and tiny, brightly colored coquina clams are the most conspicuous marine residents here.

Landward, above the reach of normal high tides, is the beach zone. A few plants, tolerant of salt-laden sand and air, begin to appear in the sand. Most of them are grasses and vines. They are vulnerable to storm tides, but they are pioneer species that, sooner or later, return to colonize the upper beaches.

Higher than the upper beach, the Sanibel dunes consist of low ridges. Dunes begin to develop when windborne sand is intercepted. Driftwood and beach plants act like fences, stopping the passage of windblown particles. As the sand particles accumulate, a dune begins to rise. Dunes are extremely important on Sanibel and other barrier islands as nature's defense against storm tides. They blunt tides and, as a sand depository, they are helpful in the natural process of beach rebuilding after storms.

Because the Sanibel dunes are some distance above normal tide lines, their vegetation is quite lush when compared to the scattered plants of the high beach. The tangles of wild plants help stabi-

*Outbound tides leave their signatures on the beach—sun-dappled wave lines and the most familiar of marine echinoderms, the common Forbes' sea star (*Asterias forbesi*). Discards of high, angry seas collect in long ribbons of beach wrack on the upper shore.*

Driftwood lies in repose on the wild sweep of Bowman's Beach, but it may not have found its final resting place. A higher sea than that which stranded the wood may roar ashore and take it on still another journey.

lize the dunes, which, otherwise, would be gradually blown inland or washed out by storms. One of the most important plants on the dunes is the stately sea oat. It is a deep-rooted plant, wonderfully adapted for growing even as sand accumulates around it.

* * *

Most of Captiva's natural dune vegetation was destroyed long ago by the construction of seaside buildings and the Sanibel-Captiva Road, and by the resulting erosion. Sanibel's natural dune vegetation is patchy: lush and vigorous where it has been left alone and scraggly or nonexistent where construction has been overbearing. Near Sanibel's Gulfside City Park is the Perry tract of the "Ding" Darling National Wildlife Refuge, a tiny parcel of dune and beach in their natural, undisturbed state. The Perry tract is covered by delightful snarls of sea grape, yucca, seaside coreopsis, sea purslane, sea oats, and wild beach grasses. Not far from the Perry tract are dunes carpeted by cultivated Bahia grass and "protected" from the sea by concrete retaining walls.

The little Perry refuge isn't the only place on Sanibel where natural beach vegetation persists. Especially at Bowman's Beach, look for mats of beach morning-glory, beach plum, sea grape, and robust clumps of sea oats on the dunes. Even along the expanse of the Bowman dunes, however, some of the indigenous plant cover has been lost. Construction wasn't the felon here; the Australian pine, or casuarina, was.

The fast-growing casuarinas of Australia were brought to Florida and planted several generations ago as ornamentals and windbreaks. They soon spread far beyond their cultivated borders and crowded out native species. Their dense foliage and floor of needles make it nearly impossible for other plants to grow underneath them.

Many people assume that the familiar, long-needled casuarina is a natural feature of Sanibel and Captiva. It is no more native than it is a pine. Although not everyone finds the trees unattractive, they have been extremely damaging to native vegetation and, consequently, to the wildlife

that depends on the vegetation. In an effort to reestablish indigenous plant species, city, county, and federal officials agree that the Australian pines belong only in Australia. A hurricane would expedite eradication of the casuarina, but it is likely that government agencies will strike first.

Animals that live on the upper beach and dune range from spiders and ants to a multitude of other invertebrates such as snakes, lizards, and the ponderous loggerhead sea turtle. The Atlantic loggerhead nests each summer in the sand above the high tide's wrack line. While the loggerhead's stay is brief, ghost crabs are permanent residents of the high beach. They are particularly active at night, slipping from their burrows and clacking over shells to forage in beach wrack.

Distant relatives of the sea turtles, gopher tortoises sometimes colonize the dunes with their woodchuck-like burrows. Tourists occasionally make the acquaintance of these grass-munching land turtles on the dunes within a few paces of the sea. Well-meaning folks assume that the gophers are sea turtles and want to return them to the ocean. That's a bit like putting an ostrich in a tree. Gopher tortoises want no part of the sea, and they should be left in the prickly, cluttered undergrowth of the dunes. If you are in doubt, gopher tortoises and sea turtles can be easily told apart. If you can pick it up, it's a gopher tortoise. Sea turtles weigh about 250 pounds and come ashore at night. Gopher tortoises weigh about four pounds and travel about by day.

Sanibel's high beach is a resting place for many species of sandpipers, terns, gulls, and black skimmers. One of the most striking of the sandpipers is the black-bellied plover, whose black and white breeding plumage makes it something of a dandy among shorebirds. The plovers and other shorebirds feed in the surf zone or pick through the wrack for tiny invertebrates. Fish crows scavenge on the beach, and many songbirds, including cardinals, great crested flycatchers, and smooth-billed anis are found on the dunes.

Several of the big wading birds loiter on the beach. Great egrets stalk the upper beach and dune edge for anoles, skinks, and snakes. Black-

Sanibel's gopher tortoises (Gopherus polyphemus) *live in colonies in sandy woodlands and on dunes, where they munch on grass and other vegetation. Tortoises take refuge in their burrows, but they often venture out during the hottest part of the day. Seaside gophers are sometimes mistaken for sea turtles and placed in the surf by well-meaning but* badly *mistaken tourists.*

legged snowy egrets, stepping on golden toes, hunt minnows in the sea wash. Great blue herons visit the sea edge day and night. Its croak and huge flight shadow give away the great blue heron's presence after dark.

A few bird species of the Sanibel-Captiva shore hunt the sea edge even when the surf runs high. White ibis, their down-curved bills probing the wash for mole crabs, wade perilously close to breakers. At the instant a wave poises to boil over, the ibis high-steps from its path. Sanderlings and ruddy turnstones are superb at trotting into the wash after a wave breaks and retreating before the next wave overruns them. Whatever the sea's rhythm, the birds master the beat.

Perhaps the finest island haunt for feeling the rhythm of the ocean is Bowman's Beach. Cross the footbridge over the old Blind Pass lagoon and walk quickly through a forest of casuarinas. The open gulf is at your feet and the tang of salt air licks your face. As far as anyone can see, left and right, is open beach. During the September low season, when tourism slackens, a visitor to Bowman's can find rare oceanfront solitude. Nothing here to intrude on the broad, wild sweep of ocean and sand save passing squadrons of brown pelicans and the whistling cries of willets.

The haunting, melodious cries of willets (Catoptrophorus semipalmatus) are as exhilarating as the birds' sand-colored plumage is dull. By day these shorebirds are most often found on the gulf beaches, where they flirt with breaking waves. This migrating flock has gathered for the night at the edge of a bay lit by a retreating sun.

UPLANDS AND
WETLANDS

Inland, well beyond the gulf shore, is an altogether different Sanibel. Here is Sanibel's midsection, a quilt of wooded ridges and wetlands. The boundaries between them are often indistinct, influenced greatly by current rainfall. Thomas Missimer's geological studies on Sanibel in the early 1970s revealed as many as 300 individual ridges. Since they rise only one to three feet above surrounding ground, they are indeed subtle features. Nevertheless, the slight differences in altitude result in many different plant associations and levels of ground moisture. The strands of relatively high, dry ground provide a foothold for a scruffy forest of shrubs and some trees. Between the ridges are depressions occupied by swales, marshes, and sloughs.

Sanibel's woodlands and interior marshes are its least-known habitats. The nonresident population reveres the beach, and thousands of people drive through the great mangrove swamp forests of the "Ding" Darling National Wildlife Refuge. Far fewer people explore the Sanibel woodlands and sloughs, although that situation is changing thanks to a system of trails in the 247-acre Sanibel-Captiva Conservation Foundation preserve in mid-island. The foundation trails cross swales, skirt the Sanibel River slough, and meander along the ridges. The well-marked trails are an excellent introduction to Sanibel's inland vegetation and wildlife.

Marshlands at the foundation preserve are flooded or wet most of the time. The water level fluctuates dramatically, however, according to the season. The wetlands are heavily grown up with cord grass, leather fern, saw grass, and various sedges. The blossoms of mallow and marsh-pink lend a blush of color.

Sloughs are wetlands characterized by bushes and trees, such as buttonwood. The sloughs usually retain some water after marshes and grassy swales lose most of their surface water in droughts. The foundation preserve protects the depressions and sloughs that help form the Sanibel River.

The freshwater wetlands are havens for a splendid variety of animals. Many of them are microorganisms or tiny invertebrates that are the basis of the wetland food chains. A number of small fish, for example, eat mosquito larva, insects, and other invertebrates. The fish are prey for larger fish, anhingas, pied-billed grebes, least bitterns, and many other animals.

The southern leopard frog and pig frog of the sloughs live mostly on an insect diet. The frogs, in turn, are eaten by the Florida watersnake, herons, and raccoons, among other predators. The champion consumer of the sloughs is the American alligator. Alligators feed largely upon fish, turtles, and water birds. Once a 'gator reaches adulthood, it no longer has any natural enemies.

The woodlands tend to have a tangled understory of wild coffee, saw palmetto, wild prickly lime, Spanish bayonet, cat's-claw, wax myrtle, rosary pea, buckthorn, Jamaica dogwood, wild

Marsh pink (Sabatia campanulata) *is one of several species of Sanibel wildflowers. Like many wildflowers, marsh pinks color roadsides, fields, and marsh edges.*

The northern cardinal (Cardinalis cardinalis), *America's beloved "redbird," whistles from Sanibel woodlands, backyards, and thickets.*

Dew beads on the leaves of sea grape (Coccoloba uvifera) *growing on a Sanibel dune. The bushy sea grape also grows inland and achieves "tree" status where it is sufficiently shielded from the rigors of ocean wind and salt spray. Jelly is sometimes made from the fruit of the sea grape.*

The ubiquitous raccoon (Procyon lotor) *is equally at home in a Sanibel cabbage palm, on the ground, or in a mangrove swamp. Although chiefly nocturnal, Sanibel raccoons often forage during the day.*

cotton, Cherokee bean, and numerous other plants. Although Sanibel is three degrees north of the Tropic of Cancer, the line of demarcation between the tropic and temperate zones, many of the island's shrubs, and at least two of its trees — the strangler fig and gumbo limbo — are of tropical, West Indian origin.

Two other prominent trees at the foundation preserve and elsewhere in the island's woods are cabbage, or sabal, palm and sea grape. The broad-leafed sea grape is typically a bush, but it can achieve tree status when it grows far enough inland to avoid the increased salt and wind of its frontal dune habitat.

Like other natural habitats on Sanibel, the wooded ridges are important to several species of wild animals. One of them is the gopher tortoise, a burrowing turtle that lives in colonies. Gopher tortoises, table food for early settlers on Sanibel, like high, dry ridges because they reduce the chances of flooded burrows. The woods seem like a curious place to find turtles, but the Florida box turtle lives here, too, traveling between upland and wetter areas. Much more common than the box turtle is another reptile, the five-lined skink. You may see this small lizard racing across your path or hear it rummaging in fallen leaves.

Among other Sanibel reptiles, alligators are the darlings of tourists. Many residents aren't nearly as fond of them. Alligators are abundant in the brackish water of the "Ding" Darling National Wildlife Refuge's main tract and its Bailey tract, but they don't necessarily stay there. Alligators are also common in the freshwater wetlands of interior Sanibel. 'Gators sometimes crawl into trouble with their human neighbors and have made themselves briefly at home in swimming pools, on screened porches, and in residential canals and ponds. In 1988, an alligator described as "a ten-footer" grabbed the leg of an elderly man as he was wading in a drainage ditch to clear weeds. The man struggled free, but as Sanibel's human population grows, there will undoubtedly be more alligator-human encounters.

If the wayward alligator is under six feet long,

a local, licensed alligator handler is called to remove it and release it elsewhere. 'Gators over six feet long are the state's responsibility.

Perhaps nothing makes people more uneasy than to see an alligator on the beach or in the gulf. The gulf isn't a regular stomping ground for 'gators, but neither are swimming pools. "Whenever someone sees an alligator in the gulf, the phones ring off the hook," said Charles LeBuff, recalling his days as an official at the national wildlife refuge.

A somewhat conspicuous avian resident of the woods is the rufous-sided towhee. A plump sparrow, the towhee rustles about on the ground for insects and seeds. Two other birds frequenting the woods are the red-bellied woodpecker and cardinal.

Many woodland animals, such as the bobcat and raccoon, are chiefly nocturnal. Others are secretive or too small and too well camouflaged to be readily apparent. Snakes — black racers, indigos, corals, and eastern diamondback rattlers — live in these woods, but they usually avoid discovery. Green and squirrel treefrogs and southern toads become active when rains thrash the island and trigger the animals' mating behavior. In fact, the calls of the treefrogs can be nearly deafening on a rainy night.

Sanibel woodlands are essentially shrub forests without true trees in the abundance, diversity, or stature associated with mainland forests. These woodlands gouge, stick, and claw at anyone who brazenly leaves a wooded path. If the forest could talk, it would undoubtedly snarl. Yet it has a saw-toothed charm, like lizards and old loggerheads with barnacles on their shells. It mirrors the rigors of harsh environmental conditions — drought, flood, intense heat, and sunshine — and lies almost within earshot of the sea and its salty winds. More important, the forest plants are rooted in sandy soil that has only a thin layer of nutritious humus. It's the kind of forest one would expect to grow, with a little nourishment, in the moon's Sea of Tranquility.

The Sanibel-Captiva Conservation Foundation tract on Sanibel-Captiva Road offers hikers a fine network of trails into Sanibel's woodlands and freshwater marshes. An observation tower provides an overview. Trails wander through stands of native vegetation like the cabbage palm (left). The cabbage, or sabal, palm (Sabal palmetto) is Florida's state tree.

Dawn strikes an emerging alligator (Alligator mississippiensis) in a Sanibel pond. Alligators are found throughout Sanibel's freshwater and brackish water wetlands. Reigning at the top of the aquatic food chains, adult alligators have no natural enemies. They typically prey upon fish, turtles, and water birds.

Lethal beauty, an eastern diamondback rattler (Crotalus adamanteus) crawls toward seaside cover. The eastern diamondback, which has reached a record ninety-six inches in length, keeps a low profile on Sanibel, preferring to hunt its prey—rodents and rabbits—in the coolness of night.

The sun sets behind a clump of red mangroves and their distinctive latticework of prop roots in the J.N. "Ding" Darling National Wildlife Refuge. Sanibel's "backside" has nearly twenty-eight hundred acres of swampy mangrove forest.

MUD AND MANGROVES: THE JUNGLED SHORE

A large portion of Sanibel's actual shoreline does not confront the Gulf of Mexico. Sanibel's other shore is its bay side, which faces the protected waters of Pine Island Sound, San Carlos Bay, and innumerable lesser inlets. The Sanibel shores of these quiet, shallow bay waters are for the most part covered by an enormous forest of mangrove trees. Such figures are hard to determine precisely, but approximately nine miles of Sanibel's nearly twenty-five miles of saltwater shore is covered by a fringe of mangroves. Also impressive is the fact that of the nearly eleven thousand acres that compose the island, twenty-eight hundred acres are in mangrove swamp. Mangroves don't cover Sanibel's entire bay side; fragments of sandy beach meet San Carlos Bay. Mangroves are, however, clearly a major component of the Sanibel environment.

The mangrove zone is at once low land and shallow bay. The distinctions between land and water constantly shift as tides ebb and flow. Almost every area where mangroves live is subject to tidal influence and many stands of mangroves are nearly always standing in salt water.

Mangroves are remarkable trees. They are halophytes, which, unlike more common trees, are salt-tolerant. The bushy mangroves thrive in salty habitats where other trees would be flat-out deadwood. Not surprisingly, mangroves play an important role in south Florida's coastal ecosystems.

Three species of tree share the common name "mangrove." They are not closely related trees taxonomically, but they fill similar ecological niches and often intermix on Sanibel and elsewhere. Generally, the red mangrove (*Rhizophora mangle*) is the most seafaring of the mangroves. It is certainly the most recognizable because it has distinctly arched prop roots. In low tides, red mangroves appear to be standing on lattices of bowlegs. During high tides, the "legs" are submerged.

Black mangroves (*Avicennia germinans*) usually live on slightly higher ground than the reds. These mangroves have a distinct feature, too. In the mud around them, black mangroves send up pneumatophores—soft, vertical shoots that apparently function as breathing aids. White mangroves (*Laguncularia racemosa*) and buttonwood (*Conocarpus erectus*), a mangrove-like species sometimes called button-mangrove, tend to live on higher, less saline ground than the red and black species.

Sanibel's mangroves lie in an extensive, discontiguous wilderness of mud and green, swampy forest. They fringe Sanibel, Captiva, Buck Key, and scores of islets that are, essentially, part of a miniature archipelago. This sodden coastal zone is endlessly contested by land and sea. Here and there, in the midst of the mangrove realm, ground has emerged barely above the reach of high tides. Often, it is a Calusa midden with its characteristic covering of gumbo limbo trees and West Indian shrubs. Below the shrubs are armies of fiddler

Overleaf: Bushy, salt-tolerant mangroves thrive in saline habitat that would kill other trees. Brown pelicans, seen here in an aerial view, nest on mangrove islets in Tarpon Bay and elsewhere in the region.

crabs and the mangroves.

The mangrove forest is a jumble of roots and branches. The forest stands in a bed of jelly-bottomed muck and shells. The tree roots trap leaves, sea grass, seaweeds, and the assorted flotsam of estuaries and bays. In the heat, wetness, and mud, the mangroves are a jungle of dark, distorted corridors. Columbus noted on his visit to the New World that the mangroves were "so thick a cat couldn't get ashore."

Unlike Columbus, Paul Moler, a herpetologist with the Florida Game and Freshwater Fish Commission, has weaved and splashed through the mangroves of Florida many times. On the rare, celebrated occasions when an American crocodile, a Moler specialty, turns up on Sanibel—in 1981 and 1989, for example—Moler hears about it. Moler has formulated a law about mangrove swamps. He says it is his law, but it reeks of Murphy. According to Moler, when you are wading through the mangrove swamp, the water is always one inch higher than your boots. He's right, of course. The mangrove jungle is best left to raccoons.

One can only imagine how the Calusas lived in the mangroves. They probably didn't wear boots. One theory about their demise is that they were carried off by mosquitoes. In any event, Calusa shell middens are scattered about on obscure islets around Sanibel and in the outer bays. They are rarely invaded, these little clumps of trees and shell. Their stillness is interrupted only by the whine of mosquitoes, the chatter of birds, and the claw-on-bark scratching of mangrove crabs.

As late as the early 1970s, the mangrove community was considered expendable on Sanibel and elsewhere in Florida. William Odum, a University of Miami marine biologist who became a leading proponent of mangrove preservation, lamented the "tendency for some scientists to dismiss such environments [mangrove ecosystems] as 'ecological curiosities' which contribute little to the animal communities of surrounding waters." Today, thanks to the original research of Odum and Eric J. Heald, we know far more about mangroves, particularly red mangroves, than we did when developers were pour-ing concrete seawalls around coastal properties. We know that the destruction of mangroves is ecologically foolish and possibly catastrophic. On Sanibel, mangroves are protected by the city, state, and federal governments. As Bill Hammond, the director of the Lee County Environmental Education program, says, "Mangroves have become almost sacred."

Odum and Heald showed that the detritus of red mangroves was the energy base for a broad and complex coastal food web. In short, mangroves are plants from which many animals derive the nourishment they convert into life-sustaining energy. The energy doesn't pass directly to the wild animal; few creatures feed on mangrove leaves, bark, and twigs until they have been processed. The energy potential of the mangrove material is unlocked after it is degraded by bacteria and fungi. Then the nutritional benefits of the mangrove work their way through the food chains.

Tiny invertebrates, which feed on microorganisms that cluster on mangrove particles, are devoured by larger marine animals. Eventually, energy once stored in mangrove trees reaches predators at the top of the food chains: wading birds, alligators, birds of prey, large fish, and, of course, humans consuming sea products.

A representative chain of life in the Sanibel mangroves may begin with a small fish. The fish obtains nutrition from the microorganisms that attack a fallen mangrove leaf and have, themselves, been nourished by the leaf. The little fish is potential prey for a legion of larger animals, including juvenile gamefish. Larger fish are game for herons, ospreys, and bald eagles. Many of the fish that Sanibel's ospreys snare are products of the mangrove community, and so, then, are the splendid ospreys themselves.

For several wild animals, the mangroves are home, roost, restaurant, or way station. Many bird species use the red and black mangroves on islands near Sanibel for roosting and nesting. This group includes wading birds, double-crested cormorants, and brown pelicans. Four songbirds—the black-whiskered vireo, mangrove cuckoo, prairie warbler, and gray

Undersea forests of marine grasses hide fish, snails, and the tasty Atlantic blue crab (Callinectes sapidus). Crabbing for the abundant blues is a popular diversion on Sanibel.

Black mangroves (Avicennia germinans) do not have the arched prop roots of red mangroves (Rhizophora mangle). In fact, the mangroves are ecologically rather than taxonomically close. Black mangroves have distinctive pneumatophores—vertical shoots that presumably aid transpiration. Black mangroves often grow in stands mixed with red mangroves and white mangroves (Laguncularia racemosa).

Mangrove-enriched bays treat Sanibel wading birds to a full breakfast when tide is low. Egrets and herons crowd the muddy flats to feast on crustaceans, fish, and other concentrated marine organisms.

kingbird—nest in Sanibel mangroves also.

Reptiles are not plentiful in mangrove swamps. With the exception of corn snakes, yellow rat snakes, and mangrove water snakes, all of which can shinny up a tree, serpents don't forsake firm ground to venture into the jungle. From a snake's point of view, hunting is poor. The wet, salty earth and lack of terrestrial vegetation discourage a rodent population, and songbird nests are scarce. Another reptile, the diamondback terrapin, likes the saltwater shallows by the mangroves. It is the only American turtle, other than the sea turtle genera, with a predilection for salt water.

With the exception of the raccoon and possibly otters, mammals rarely enter Sanibel's mangroves. Marsh rabbits, bobcats, and opossums are passersby. The raccoon, which can adapt to any habitat short of law school, has no problem with the special difficulties of foraging and finding passage among the mangroves. One of the raccoon's favorite foods is the coon oyster, a mollusk that attaches itself to the prop roots of red mangroves.

The shallow undersea habitat of the bays that nourish Sanibel mangroves is easily explored at low tide. Dark green forests of waving turtle grass blades lie almost under the shadows of shoreline mangroves. Many fascinating animals, all of them linked to mangrove and marine grass food chains, live in this kingdom of mud and grass and roots. The quicksilver glint of fish—sea trout, pipefish, mackerel, redfish, ladyfish—is everywhere. Blue crabs and predatory sea snails, the lightning whelks, crown conchs, Florida horse conchs, pear whelks, and tulips prowl the bottom. Sea urchins, nudibranches, octopus, miniature seahorses, marine worms, oysters, and the strange sea hare, a mollusk without a shell, live here. Clams and colonies of fragile, white angel's wings, a favorite of shell collectors, live in the muddy sand.

But that is just a sampling of the wealth of marine animals in the shallow bays. Even Lee County's environmental education publication, which includes 175 bay species, is not an exhaustive guide. The health of Sanibel's mangrove coast and bay water has far-reaching implications for wildlife and people alike. Sanibel's surf side isn't its only treasured coast.

Above: A familiar sight in the Sanibel skies, the magnificent osprey, or fish hawk (Pandion haliaetus), sweeps onto a top-less cabbage palm to feed on its catch, a flounder. The osprey lives exclusively on fish, which it catches with its talons. Mangrove food chains provide a healthy fish stock. **Left:** Jumbled red mangrove branches are a favorite roost for birds like the white ibis (Eudocimus albus). The Wildlife Drive auto route and foot trails in the J.N. "Ding" Darling National Wildlife Refuge lead visitors to close encounters with mangroves and the wildlife that lives among them.

First light of day illuminates a great blue heron (Ardea herodias), standing like a four-foot lawn statue on Sanibel's northernmost shore. Although not usually nocturnal, hungry great blues, largest of the American herons, often prowl Sanibel's beaches on moonlit nights. The bird's croak and shadowy flight have startled many a turtle watcher.

TURTLE TRACKS

Charles LeBuff has lived on Sanibel Island since 1958. He may be the only resident ever who can claim to have spent more nights than days on Sanibel's gulf beaches. LeBuff's excuse is simple: turtles. For more than twenty years, LeBuff has been watching, studying, and tagging the Atlantic loggerhead sea turtles that crawl onto Sanibel beaches. And because loggerheads nest at night, LeBuff knows more about darkness than Dracula.

LeBuff is a first-rate naturalist, but he's always had a special soft spot for the crusty loggerhead. In 1968 he founded Caretta Research and began with several associates on both Florida coasts to systematically study the loggerhead, the only sea turtle that commonly nests in Florida. In 1990 LeBuff published a monograph of his studies, *The Loggerhead Turtle in the Eastern Gulf of Mexico*.

If it is incomprehensible that someone should aid and protect a hard, cold-blooded animal with a brain the size of a small lettered olive shell, consider the late Dr. Archie Carr's affliction with sea turtles. Dr. Carr, a preeminent sea turtle authority, spoke for more than a few folks when he explained, "I was drawn to sea turtles partly because . . . there were gross blank pieces in their natural history, partly because I saw a hawksbill come ashore out of a phosphorescent surf one night and dig in the sand while a thin moon climbed."

Loggerheads don't always come ashore on moonlit nights, but whenever they come ashore, they leave a telltale track that looks like a small tractor's. To find turtles, LeBuff drives Bowman's Beach in an open vehicle. He doesn't necessarily look for a turtle on the beach. More often he sees the turtle's track where none had been before. A turtle may still be a dark lump on the high beach, or she may have already nested and looped back into the sea. She may also have crawled ashore, changed her mind, and crawled back into the surf. You don't have to be a Calusa to read these tracks.

By chance, night walkers on Sanibel and Captiva occasionally find a nesting loggerhead. Most people who see loggerheads on Sanibel are with LeBuff, who has taken hundreds of people on his nightly forays during the May through August nesting season. Mysteries about the loggerhead's life cycle at sea abound, but their nesting behavior is well documented. One researcher quipped that he saw more Ph.D.s on his study beach than turtles.

If someone needs a reason, looking for a loggerhead on a midsummer's night is a good one for prowling the night beach. Anticipation and antiquity linger in the humid air. Phosphorescence gleams on unruly waves. Night herons, startled by the slow-rolling vehicle, squawk as they flap to more private digs further down the beach. But prying with night eyes into the dark, looking for a turtle out of its customary element, is more than a novel reason for being on the beach. It's a window to Mesozoic times, which predate the historic Sanibel lighthouse by about 90 million years.

It was then, some scientists contend, during the

Sanibel's high beach is a traditional nesting ground for the Atlantic loggerhead turtle (Caretta caretta caretta). A female loggerhead may nest several times during the season. One loggerhead laid 917 eggs in six nesting forays to Sanibel shores in 1973.

Age of Dinosaurs, that the loggerhead's forebears first crawled onto moon-dappled beaches to dig their nest holes. Along the evolutionary way, the big boys vanished. The sea turtles, albeit with modifications, survived. Today, remarkably enough, one can still be privy to the spectacle of a giant reptile from the sea nesting on a Sanibel beach.

With its lightweight, streamlined shell and paddle-like flippers, the loggerhead is adapted for life at sea. It sleeps, mates, feeds, and spends virtually its entire life at sea. Adult males, so far as is known, never come ashore. The loggerhead has evolved large pectoral muscles necessary for powering its breaststroke. The muscle bulk occupies space that might otherwise be a compartment for the withdrawal of the turtle's head and neck. Don't expect a nesting loggerhead to shyly tuck in its head; the head stays out. Adult loggerheads nesting in Florida average about 225 pounds. Specimens over 300 pounds are unusual, but 500- and 800-pound loggerheads have been recorded.

Prior to laying eggs, about 110 of them, the turtle scoops a bulb-shaped nest in the sand with her hind flippers. Her eggs, like slick, leathery golfballs, tumble from her ovipositor into the nest. During a nesting season, a loggerhead may nest several times. In 1973 LeBuff found one turtle that had dug six nests and laid 917 eggs on Sanibel. When the laying is finished, the loggerhead uses her hind flippers like hands to cover the eggs with sand. Sweeps of her fore flippers obliterate the nest site, but her tractor-crawl signature leaves a trail to the nest area.

A loggerhead's life as mom lasts only as long as she's on the beach—about an hour. Her departure is unhurried and subject to frequent pauses for breath. When she finally reaches the moist line of crushed shells at the edge of the sea, her ordeal as a terrestrial creature ends. The lip of a wave splashes across her head. Spirit renewed, she slips into the surf and disappears.

There is no guarantee that the eggs will survive and hatch. Loggerhead nests mistakenly dug too low on the beach will be swamped. Violent

Having covered her clutch, a loggerhead returns to the buoyancy and safety of the Gulf of Mexico. The entire pilgrimage ashore usually takes the turtle about an hour. Male loggerheads never go ashore.

storms can wreck even well-placed nests on the high beach. Probing sea oat roots and predators, mostly ghost crabs and raccoons, ruin a few more nests. Over the years, LeBuff and other researchers have carefully moved some clutches from sure disaster and relocated them in natural sand chambers.

Fifty-five to sixty days after the eggs are laid, tiny loggerheads emerge from the nest after dark, usually between ten o'clock and midnight. The hatchlings, each less than two inches long, erupt in a swarm. The turtles steer a fast course directly to the sea and apparently find the ocean unerringly because they are responsive to light. Under natural conditions, the seaward horizon is almost always brighter than the landward horizon. As one can imagine, sea turtle hatchlings can be easily disoriented by beach lights.

The youngsters may be grabbed on their first night out by herons, ghost crabs, or raccoons. If they reach the ocean safely, they may be preyed upon by fish. The few turtles that do reach adulthood are quite safe from natural enemies with the

exceptions of sharks and certain marine parasites. In recent years, the loggerheads' most lethal adversaries have been shrimp boats, whose nets inadvertently capture loggerheads. Tangled or otherwise unable to reach the surface for air, the turtles drown. However, the shrimping fleet is increasing its use of turtle excluder devices (TEDs) mandated by the federal government, which seems to have brought about a sharp reduction in marine turtle deaths. Ultimately, a greater total loggerhead population may result in a larger number of loggerheads nesting on Sanibel and Captiva.

In the late 1950s, LeBuff counted 220 nests one season on a nine-mile stretch of Sanibel. A similar census turned up just seventy nests in 1970 as beachfront development intensified. But the number of nests has increased since then, and it has been fairly stable between 120 and 140. Landowners have helped the turtles by either dimming or extinguishing their shorefront lights during the nesting season.

About eight weeks after being buried in the sand, loggerhead eggs hatch at night. Unless they are distracted by lights, hatchling turtles rush unerringly for the ocean and vanish in the surf.

Aptly christened, the ghost crab (Ocypode quadrata) blends with its sandy environment. Secretive by day, these burrowing crustaceans emerge at night to clatter over beach wrack in a search of food. A ghost crab can overpower and kill a baby loggerhead.

The yellow-crowned night heron (Nyctanassa violacea) *shows off breeding plumes each March when wooing a mate. This heron's elaborate courtship can sometimes be seen at close range in the J.N. "Ding" Darling National Wildlife Refuge. Night herons see well in low light and usually begin their hunts as the diurnal herons fly to their roosts. Occasionally, night herons spear hatchling loggerheads.*

A pair of roseate spoonbills (Ajaia ajaja) rest in the tidal shallows of the Darling refuge. Sanibel is one of the spoonbill's strongholds in Florida. Once nearly extirpated from the state, spoonbills have gradually rebounded and nest as far north as Tampa Bay. Although they don't nest in the Sanibel area, they can be seen year-round on the island.

A FLURRY OF WINGS

A primary reason for visiting Sanibel Island is to observe wildlife. More often than not, wildlife on Sanibel means birds. Sanibel Island is arguably one of the three best sites in Florida for the observation of water birds close-up. Naturally, some times are better for viewing than others. The tides, time of day, and the season of the year all influence the abundance and variety of birds.

Sanibel is an ornithological candy store for several reasons, not the least of which is the protected land of the "Ding" Darling National Wildlife Refuge. But Sanibel geography is as propitious as Sanibel protection. Lying toward the southern end of the Florida peninsula, the island is a terminus for many migratory birds along the Atlantic flyway. As an outlying barrier island, it is also a convenient stopover for migrants and a haven for storm-blown birds. And several different habitats—beach, dune, freshwater wetland, coastal ridge woodland, and mangrove swamp—in a relatively small area attract a large number of species. A checklist of birds sighted at least twice on Sanibel or nearby between 1974 and 1984 included 247 species. Another forty-four species are accidentals—occurring only occasionally. Sixty-three species nest in the area. The Sanibel-Captiva Audubon Society, in cooperation with the National Audubon Society, annually conducts a count of birds on Sanibel and Captiva on one day in late December. Almost every year, the count exceeds 110 species.

About forty of the Sanibel bird species are on federal or state lists of birds that are judged to be endangered, threatened, rare, or of special concern. Among them are the bald eagle (threatened), roseate spoonbill (rare), wood stork (endangered), and black-crowned night heron (special concern).

Avid bird observers armed with spotting scopes and field glasses spend most of their time keying on the main tract of the national wildlife refuge. Many of the birds there are habituated to slow-moving cars, so they are tolerant of nearby watchers and photographers. More important for bird enthusiasts, most of the 247 birds on the checklist have been seen in the refuge proper at one time or another.

The Bailey tract of the refuge, which is separate from the main Darling tract, is another prime location for birds. It has several wetland habitats and enough shrub and swale to make it attractive to waders, shorebirds, and passerines. In the spring and summer, the Bailey tract's most fetching resident is the black-necked stilt, a shorebird pied in black and white. A busy hunter of aquatic and semi-aquatic insects, the stilt is known for its spindly red legs.

Birds are plentiful along the beach, too, especially when people aren't. During the fall and spring migrations, bird observation is particularly worthwhile along Bowman's Beach, at the Blind Pass inlet, and at Point Ybel by the Sanibel light.

Some of the most spectacular water birds gather together to nest at rookeries in the island's wetlands and on nearby mangrove islets. Rookeries of nesting herons, cormorants, and brown pelicans are smelly, chaotic places. One little mangrove island can be colonized each spring and summer by as many as a half dozen or more species of water birds, and one species or another may occupy the island from February through August with nesting and rearing its young.

These little colonies are crowded with birds. Territorial squabbles are commonplace. A brown pelican that carelessly touches down too close to a nesting double-crested cormorant will attract threatening gestures — an arched neck and mouth agape. A great egret in plumed splendor will draw the thrust of its neighbor's bill if it approaches too closely. From every nook of these islands come rasps, grunts, croaks, and the rush of wings.

Amid the confusion is a semblance of order. The larger species nest on the upper and outermost limbs, such choice waterfront locations assisting them in quick launches. Smaller species, such as snowy egrets and black-crowned night herons, nest on lower and interior branches. Another aspect of orderliness involves staggered nesting. Not all species begin their courtship, mating, and nest-building at the same time. Consequently, the young of these colonial nesting species hatch over an extended time rather than all at once. When great blue herons fledge in March or April, for example, several other species have just begun nesting. Staggered nesting helps protect fish populations in concentrated areas, but it also makes food procurement easier for adult birds when they have fewer other adults with which to compete for fish supplies.

Sanibel is a fine spot for bird study as well as observation. A quiet watcher by a bay in the refuge can observe how Sanibel's wading birds have adapted to somewhat distinct ecological niches. The great egrets and great blue herons fish in the deepest water, the prize for having the longest legs. The reddish egret and Louisiana heron, both medium-sized waders, stay in shallower water. The small green-backed heron often hunts from a snag over the water. Night herons fill another niche. They usually begin hunting at dusk, when the diurnal waders stream to their roosts.

The reddish egret is the most entertaining of the heron tribe. It rushes about, wings outstretched, in the shallows. Such behavior belies the patient stalking technique of most waders. Sooner or later the reddish egret succeeds in panicking a school of baitfish into its path.

The anhinga, or snakebird, hunts fish by spearing them with its bill underwater. It doesn't have the usual complement of natural preening oil to waterproof its feathers, so the anhinga sinks easily. The down side for the anhinga is that it becomes waterlogged. After a hunt, it has to perch with its wings outstretched to dry. The double-crested cormorant, a close relative, tends to hunt in deeper water, usually sea water. Both of these birds can be seen in characteristic "drying" poses on mangroves in the refuge.

One of the most unusual adaptations among Sanibel avifauna is the flat, spatula-shaped bill of the roseate spoonbill. The spoonbill is an active hunter of fish, little mollusks and crustaceans, usually in saltwater bays. As it walks, the spoonbill swings its bill through the water, all the while opening and closing its mandibles. The mandibles are sensitized and grooved, and they clamp shut when they touch prey. Wood storks drag their lower mandibles through the water to locate prey in a similar, but much more deliberate fashion. White ibis have narrow, sharply curved bills, which they use to probe sand and mud for tiny aquatic animals. The black skimmer has a longer mandible on the bottom than it does on the top. As it flies, the skimmer touches the lower bill to water, leaving a knife-like wake. The bill snaps shut when it strikes a small fish. If it weren't for the friction of mandible against water, the lower bill would grow to enormous length.

One of the most popular birds of Sanibel skies and piers is the brown pelican. When they are not panhandling at docks, brown pelicans catch their own fish by making spectacular dives into the gulf and bay. Although a drab bird during the late summer and fall, an adult brown pelican undergoes a remarkable molt during the breeding season. Its head and neck are feathered in various, changing combinations of yellow, white, and brown.

The brown pelican's larger relative, the Ameri-

Early morning and a low tide in the J.N. "Ding" Darling National Wildlife Refuge invariably make an ideal partnership for birds—and bird-watchers. Few places rival Sanibel's wealth of bird life. Nearly three hundred species have been recorded in the region.

This ruddy turnstone (Arenaria interpres) on Sanibel's gulf beach wintered on the island. Now in spring plumage, this little shorebird will be northbound within days to nest on the arctic tundra.

One of the medium-sized herons, this Louisiana heron (Hydranassa tricolor) *in breeding plumage strides into a brackish water marsh. Like reddish egrets, Louisiana herons often chase their minnow prey.*

can white pelican, winters in the bays of the islands, and a few nonbreeding birds summer in Charlotte Harbor. The white pelican's feeding strategy is much different than the brown's. White pelicans swim in a flotilla, herding fish into an ever-tightening noose of pelicans. With their prey encircled, the pelicans dip their huge bills into the water and trap fish in their pouches. Like brown pelicans, they lift their heads slowly, draining water from the pouch before swallowing.

One of the magnificent predatory birds of the islands is the fish hawk, or osprey. It is just one of nineteen birds of prey on the Sanibel checklist, but it is easily the most conspicuous in behavior and abundance. Ospreys live strictly on fish, which they catch by diving. Whereas the brown pelican traps fish with its gular pouch, the osprey crashes into the sea feet first and snares a fish on sharply curved talons. Having impaled a fish, the osprey immediately taxis and flies directly to its favorite feeding perch. About fifty pairs of ospreys nest on Sanibel, many of them utilizing

artificial platforms. During a normal nesting season, each pair raises, on the average, one young to adulthood.

Sanibel resident and naturalist George Campbell, with the help of several other interested people, began building nesting platforms on Sanibel in the late 1970s. Mark "Bird" Westall, a Sanibel City Council member and ardent conservationist, later took over the program to erect nesting platforms. Westall explains that the program was started to help avoid conflict between humans and birds. Ospreys were building their heavy nests of sticks on utility poles and creating power outages as well as the potential for electrocuting themselves. Later, carefully placed nesting platforms helped dissuade ospreys from also attempting to build nests on chimneys and TV antennas.

Thanks to the efforts of Campbell, Westall, and several other Sanibel residents, the osprey population has surged, and conflict with the interests of people has declined. "We could maintain a huge capacity of ospreys here," says Westall, somewhat wistfully, "but human tolerance will be reached before the island's capacity for the birds is." Residents, on the whole, enjoy ospreys, Westall says, but some landowners don't appreciate the fish dinner scraps that ospreys leave beneath their feeding perches in human residential areas. Some residents also complain about ospreys "using their backyards for a bathroom," Westall says. Even on Sanibel, where a policy of coexistence with wild animals has been generally embraced, neatness apparently counts.

The bald eagle is essentially a seafaring bird and fish eater, too, but it doesn't share the osprey's tolerance for human activity. Southwest Florida is a stronghold for the national bird, yet Sanibel has never been a popular eagle nesting site because it lacks the tall, sturdy trees that eagles prefer. Even so, a pair of eagles nested—or tried to nest—on Sanibel through most of the 1980s and into the 1990s. Quite out of character, this pair nested alternately in a flimsy Australian pine and on a platform built for ospreys. Eagles rarely build nests on artificial platforms, but Westall suggests that the reason for that may simply be that no one has attempted to make a platform particularly suited to an eagle's ecological requirements.

Of the dozens of bird species found on Sanibel, the roseate spoonbill has become the island's favorite. Many tourists, when they cross the Sanibel bridge, don't know a spoonbill from a flamingo. But a day or two on the island converts many people to the wonders of Sanibel bird life, especially its "pink birds." People flock into the refuge each evening just before sunset to watch the flights of spoonbills. For some people, it's a social ritual, replete with open tailgates and open coolers. For others, it's strictly an ornithological experience.

South Florida's water bird populations have been in decline in recent years, and the trend has been noted on Sanibel by such competent observers as Westall and LeBuff. However, Sanibel's spoonbill population, which fluctuates upward in the warm months, is stable, much to the relief of anyone who has ever seen a spoonbill. The Sanibel birds have presumably migrated north

A black-necked stilt (Himantopus mexicanus) *casts a mirror image in a Bailey tract pond. The J.N. "Ding" Darling National Wildlife Refuge's Bailey tract is a favorite haunt for the stilt, one of sixty-three bird species that nest in the Sanibel area.*

A relative of the anhinga, the double-crested cormorant (Phalacrocorax auritus) *also spreads its wings to dry. The cormorant and anhinga sometimes share hunting lagoons on Sanibel. Generally, the cormorant spends much of its time hunting at sea, where it dives for fish.*

61

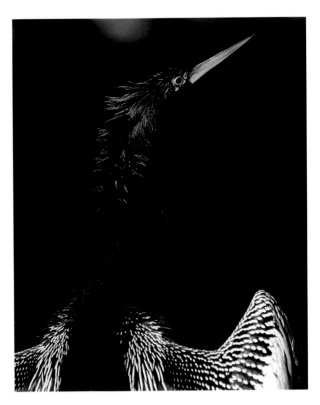

Known also as the snakebird or water turkey, an anhinga (Anhinga anhinga), in this case a male, strikes an open-winged pose characteristic of the species. An anhinga compensates for inadequate waterproofing oil on its feathers by spreading its saturated wings to dry after an underwater fishing trip.

Black skimmers (Rynchops nigra) wing past the Sanibel shore. The skimmer fishes by dragging its lower mandible like a knife through the water. Upon contact with a fish, the lower mandible snaps the fish into the skimmer's mouth.

from nesting colonies in the upper Florida Keys, Everglades National Park, and perhaps Cuba. The closest spoonbill nesting occurs in Tampa Bay. Eventually spoonbills may nest again in southwest Florida, as they did prior to the great slaughter of plume birds in the late 1800s and early 1900s. Ironically, spoonbills weren't the targets of plume hunters, but as the bird colonies were raided by egret hunters, the spoonbills abandoned their nests in the melee. The spoonbill population collapsed. By 1920 there were more confirmed reports of flying saucers in Florida than nesting spoonbills.

Charles LeBuff has seen the spoonbills at the refuge come and go. "The spoonbills are here on Sanibel year-around now," he says. "Twenty-five or thirty years ago they left in October and came back in March. Now there are over twenty here in mid-January." One June, LeBuff counted 343 spoonbills on the refuge, and he may not have seen all of them. Sanibel's summer population represents a major percentage of the entire Florida population of roseate spoonbills.

Pink spoonbills and fire-colored water make sunsets in the refuge magical times. The late sun, skulking near the fringe of distant mangroves, can burnish the water or turn it wine-red. On one such evening in March, a reddish egret, wings cupped, feathers ruffled, splashed after minnows in the shallow water near the observation tower. Moments later three roseate spoonbills banked in so low one could hear the *whoosh* of their wingbeats. They landed near the egret and began to preen. Soon another little flock of spoonbills wheeled in by the first. The egret took off as still more spoonbills arrived, their landings touching off bright circles in the glassy water.

The water blazed for a few moments while the pink birds queued up in silhouette. Then, too quickly, the sun slipped behind the mangroves and the fire on the water burned out.

The roseate spoonbill's spatula-shaped mandibles may be unwieldy for preening, but they are efficient clasps for small fish and marine crustaceans. Highly sensitized, the spoonbill's mandibles clamp on prey as the bird sweeps rapidly from side to side in shallow water. The island's only pink birds, the spoonbills are often identified as flamingoes. Wild flamingoes do not live in Florida except as accidental wanderers.

Bottle-nosed porpoises, or dolphins (Tursions truncatus), *are a common sight along the Gulf of Mexico and in Sanibel's bays. Streamlined like a shark and sharing the shark's distinctive dorsal fin, the porpoise is nevertheless one of the cetaceans, a group of highly aquatic mammals including the whales.*

MAMMALS OF SHORE AND SEA

Sanibel's birds overshadow its resident mammals. Birds are considerably more numerous and conspicuous than the island's mammals. Nevertheless, several fascinating mammals live on Sanibel and in its offshore waters. Nearly half of the thirty-four species of land mammals that live in south Florida are indigenous to Sanibel.

The most widespread of the native terrestrial mammals are the raccoon and marsh rabbit. Intelligent and omnivorous, the raccoon is one of the most adaptable mammals in North America. Raccoons have prospered on Sanibel and Captiva and elsewhere even when their wild habitats have been modified by development. On Sanibel, raccoons forage from beach to bay. They can make a living in woodlands, marshes, mangroves, and residential areas. A raccoon can gather palm fruit, dig up a fresh loggerhead nest, or use its amazingly tactile paws to pry open a garbage pail lid.

Marsh rabbits belong to the same genus as the familiar cottontail. The eastern cottontail lives in peninsular Florida but not on Sanibel or Captiva; ocean voyages are not its strong suit. Marsh rabbits are similar to cottontails in size and overall appearance. They have smaller ears, feet, and tails, however, and the underside of a marsh rabbit's tail is brown instead of white.

On the islands, marsh rabbits are found in the vegetation at the edges of wetlands, both freshwater and mangrove. They eat a variety of plants, and they are often seen stuffing their mouths with greens along Wildlife Drive in the main refuge and along foot paths through the Bailey tract. Other creatures—among them hawks, owls, eastern diamondback rattlesnakes, indigo snakes, and bobcats—may be seen stuffing their mouths with marsh rabbits.

In contrast to their cottontail kin, marsh rabbits swim well when necessary. They are not truly aquatic, but they can float like an alligator with only nose and eyes protruding from the water. Nineteenth-century naturalist John Bachman kept a pet marsh rabbit and said the beast spent hours at a time in a water trough.

Another island mammal with a fondness for water is the river otter, the same beautifully furred otter that lives throughout much of North America. Bright-eyed, whiskered, apparently playful, the otter begs to be anthropomorphized as an amiable rogue. In fact, otters may very well play; it's hard to divine the otter's behavioral motives. But the otter is indisputably a carnivore, a predator of the Sanibel ponds, canals, and sloughs where it hunts frogs, fish, and other small animals.

Otters are bundles of gusto; they seem to attack every activity, whether it is playing, swimming, or eating, with unabashed vitality. Poised at the rim of a marsh pond, an otter, never the master of poolside etiquette, takes only two minutes to loudly chomp and tear its way through a sunfish snack. The otter acts as though each crackling bite has more lip-smacking goodness than the preceding bite. The fish, grasped in the otter's front

With its prehensile tail, a baby Virginia opossum (Didelphis virginiana) *swings from a branch in a Sanibel woodland. North America's only marsupial, the 'possum carries its newborn in a pouch.*

A river otter (Lutra canadensis) munches on a sunfish snack. A prized member of Sanibel's wetland communities, the river otter is related to the weasels, skunks, marten, mink, fisher, sea otter, and other members of the musk-bearing Mustelidae family.

paws, quickly disappears in a shower of scales. A quick lick of the paws and the otter, dark and oil-slick, slips back into the pond where other snacks wait to be pursued.

Otters are probably not common on Sanibel, although it is difficult to tell with certainty. They often hunt in the most jungled and out-of-the-way wetlands, so they are rarely glimpsed. Also rarely noticed are two rodents that are quite special to the islands, the endemic Sanibel Island marsh rice rat (*Oryzomys palustris sanibeli*) and the Captiva Island cotton rat (*Sigmodon hispidus insulicola*). These two native rats should not be confused with exotic rats, such as the roof and Norway rats, which have followed people into their homes all over the globe. The cotton rat and rice rat live in the wild; they are not home invaders. The cotton rat inhabits cordgrass, brushlands, and grassy fields. The rice rat prefers wetter areas. Between these two native rats, the rice rat is more typically rat-like in appearance. The cotton rat has the short ears and twinkling eyes of a hamster.

Both of these rodents have extremely limited ranges, the result of having evolved in the more or less isolated habitats of islands. The Sanibel Island marsh rice rat has been found only on Sanibel and Captiva. The Captiva Island cotton rat lives on Captiva, Sanibel, Pine Island, Little Pine Island, and in at least one locale on the mainland near Englewood. Neither of the rats, each a race or subspecies of mainland forms, has been listed as officially endangered by the state of Florida. However, if researchers ever bother to study rats, they may find that both of these species have only marginal populations.

Visitors to the islands learn quickly that the biggest mammals in these parts live offshore. One of the most frequently seen mammals is the bottle-nosed porpoise or dolphin, the common species of porpoise in coastal Florida. They can be seen in rolling groups, or pods, in the waves off Sanibel and Captiva beaches. The porpoise is a small-toothed whale, one of the aquatic mammals known as cetaceans. Like other cetaceans, the porpoise has front limbs modified into flippers, a dorsal fin, horizontal tail flukes, and a torpedo shape. At least eleven species of cetaceans have been identified in Sanibel's adjacent waters, including Atlantic killer whales (orcas), false killer whales, pilot whales, and Atlantic right whales.

Another aquatic mammal of coastal Sanibel is the West Indian manatee. There are far more manatees pictured on Florida license plates than there are manatees. Manatee mugs on license plates are evidence of growing concern for the welfare of these docile, gray hulks, which are endangered. Each year, dozens of manatees, lolling near the surface of estuaries and bays, are maimed or killed by the props of powerboats. Disturbance by increased boat traffic has also been a factor in their decline.

Sometimes called a sea cow, the manatee vaguely looks like a walrus without tusks. The walrus is a pinniped though, one of the seals, and it comes ashore to calve, mate, and be mellow. Manatees are sirens, a thoroughly aquatic group distinguished by their paddle-like forelimbs, a tail modified to be a horizontal fin, and no dorsal fin or hind limbs.

Manatees are trusting, slow-moving creatures that feed on aquatic vegetation—up to one hundred pounds of it per day. Not surprisingly, an adult manatee can weigh nearly two thousand pounds. It is a harmless animal, but because of its bulk, a manatee startled into motion can upset a canoe. On an early morning paddle, when Tarpon Bay lies unrippled, you may see the sleek, low rise of a manatee's back above the water's plane. Remember that hidden under the surface lies the rest of the siren, as much as nineteen hundred pounds and fifteen feet of it!

Above: Sanibel's endangered West Indian manatee (Trichechus manatus), *also called the sea cow, is one of the sirens, a group of aquatic mammals. Docile and slow moving, manatees have been victimized by powerboat propellers.* **Left:** *Marsh rabbits* (Sylvilagus palustris) *are frequently seen along paths near wetlands in the J.N. "Ding" Darling National Wildlife Refuge. Related to cottontails, marsh rabbits have shorter hind legs and tails, and they are quick to swim.*

THE COAST OF SEASHELLS

Costa de Carocles—Coast of Seashells. Such was a sixteenth-century term, apparently coined by Juan Ponce de León, for Sanibel, Captiva, and Cayo Costa. Although Ponce de León's terminology was forgotten over time as each island independently evolved an identity, the Spaniard's observation is still appropriate nearly four centuries later.

Carocles are no more plentiful anywhere in Florida than on Sanibel Island. The promise of Sanibel seashells was the staff of the island's fledgling tourist industry early in the twentieth century. And somewhere along the path to the twenty-first century, serious collectors and students of seashells—conchologists—determined that in the entire Western Hemisphere there was probably no other beach as shell-rich as Sanibel. Seashells became the essence of the island's mystique and the foundation of its prominence as a tourist destination.

Sanibel's fame is not a consequence of its being a haven for rare and endemic shells. None of the four hundred or so shell species that wash onto Sanibel beaches is endemic. They are the same marine mollusks that live elsewhere in southwest Florida and, in many cases, throughout the warm seas of the Southeast. But Sanibel may very well have greater concentrations of these shells than nearby beaches. Sanibel is probably landfall for greater numbers of rare shells too, and the island's gently tapered gulf shore seems to cushion shells and assist them in arriving unbroken, a plus for a shell gatherer.

Sanibel's atypical positioning—its long east-west axis—is influential in the steady deposition of shells on the island. The island's boomerang shape makes it something of a fortuitous junction for gulf currents, which leave Sanibel awash in shells.

The empty shell one collects on a Sanibel beach was once occupied by a living mollusk, an invertebrate with a soft body that secreted a limy shell. If the shell in hand is a single, coiled shell, such as a conch, it is a univalve or gastropod. If the shell has—or had—two matching parts, like a clam, it is a bivalve, each shell being called a "valve." Bivalves are also known as pelecypods. In either case, univalve or bivalve, the shell was a product of coastal food chains. Where these food chains are healthy and productive, the animals that make up the food chain are plentiful. The shallow bottoms of Sanibel shores are nourished and enriched with the nutrients of mangroves, sea grass, and other marine organisms. The favorable habitat conditions create a fertile nursery for the marine mollusks that every child knows as seashells.

Children find seashell collecting on Sanibel beaches great fun. After all, there is an inexhaustible supply of beach shells. Shells lie strewn in ribbons, clustered in great banks, and randomly scattered. Most of them are chipped or fractured, but flaws matter not to a six-year-old.

Many adults take shell collecting more seriously. Even on Sanibel, perfect shells of many popu-

The prized junonia (Scaphella junonia) *is among Sanibel's most beautiful and rare shells. Collectors sometimes find them cast ashore by storm tides.*

lar species are elusive, especially during the peak tourist season from late December through mid-April. Some collectors dodge the competition by shelling at dawn, snorkeling, using flashlights at night, and being selective about when and where they shell. When does a knowledgable shell collector prowl the Sanibel beaches?

"It's a simple decision," says Sanibel conchologist Alice Anders. "Of course, you go after a winter storm, and you go at low tide. You don't do anything on Sanibel that has to do with marine life unless you have a tide chart."

Many people are uncomfortable handling living marine life. A live univalve with the writhing snail poking its head, antennae, and glistening-wet body out is disconcerting to the squeamish. Most people are content to beachcomb for shells. Except after storms, beach shells are vacant, which helps explain why they washed ashore in the first place. Living mollusks have places they would rather be than the beach.

Beachcombers find shells in almost infinite variety. Many of them bear names expressive of their color or configuration: calico scallop, heart cockle, bubble shell, turkey wing, yellow cockle, Chinese alphabet, sailor's ear, banded tulip, lettered olive, lightning whelk, tiger's eye, buttercup, fan shell, and a bucketful or two of others.

Storms invariably do toss live shells onto the beaches. Once upon a time they were subject to beachcombers' gluttony, but efforts encouraging moderation in the collection of live shells on Sanibel have begun to show profit. "It's a joy to see the number of people who pick up live, stranded shells and toss them back into the ocean," Anders says. "The education that has come about is just wonderful."

Serious collectors and curious tourists alike often hire a shelling guide to help them find specimens. Some twenty to thirty guides with boats are available for half- or full-day shell trips out of Sanibel and Captiva. Most shell parties, but not all, are seeking live shells. No live shells may be taken in the waters of the "Ding" Darling National Wildlife Refuge, but two live shells of each species, per person, may be taken in Sanibel waters outside the refuge. Sanibel limits don't apply to

Cayo Costa and Captiva. Shelling boats usually anchor on the backside of Sanibel, at Upper Captiva, or on Cayo Costa.

Finding live shells and a myriad of other marine invertebrates in the mud and turtle grass beds is exciting in the sense that sport fishing is; one never knows just what the catch will be. Live shellers typically find banded tulips, lightning whelks, crown conchs, Florida horse conchs, pear whelks, and perhaps lettered olives or angel's wings in muddy sand. Like sport anglers, many shellers are content to examine their shell discoveries, perhaps photograph them, and plop them back into the water. Some charters operate that way. They gladly show clients living shells and their habitat, but collecting is strictly limited to empty shells.

What shell collecting has or has not done to Sanibel's shell population over the years is the subject of some debate, and no one knows for certain. Certainly, the competition for choice shells on the beach is greater than ever, and some bay crannies have been shelled to excess. Some shellers note especially a scarcity of big Florida horse conchs. The largest snail on the Atlantic coast, it reaches nineteen inches in length and feeds on smaller gastropods.

"I really believe," says Alice Anders, "there are as many shells as there ever were. Since we've gotten our law passed [the city of Sanibel's two-per-species limit], I find many more live shells than I ever did before." Charles LeBuff concurs. "It boggles the mind how productive those animals are," says LeBuff. "I'm not sure there aren't as many now as there ever were." On the other hand, the Sanibel Live Shelling Committee published a handout in 1984 that said, "There are uncounted new shells deposited each day on our shores, but they have decreased dramatically as their breeding stock has been plundered, and they may disappear entirely unless the taking of live shells is drastically reduced."

The state of Florida recently moved in the direction of live-shell management. The state now prohibits live shell collecting without a salt-water fishing license. Collectors who go with licensed guides are exempted. Critics say the law

The rare lion's paw (Lyropecten nodosus) is a favorite of Sanibel shell collectors. Over four hundred shell species wash onto the Sanibel sands, but few trigger the excitement that a lion's paw arouses.

This true tulip shell (Fasciolaria tulipa) is occupied by the living mollusk within. The hard, sharp shield at the extended end of the animal is the operculum. By extending its body, the tulip can inch forward on the sea bottom.

Coquinas (Donax variabilis) *live in the turbulent surf zone at the edge of the sea. Like fingerprints, no two coquinas are alike in their colorful designs.*

is unenforceable and doesn't effectively limit collecting. They would prefer a total ban on live shelling, at least in select areas. Such a move would not be setting a precedent. California, Oregon, and Florida itself (John Pennekamp Coral Reef State Park) have established some inviolate marine preserves.

The native shells that collectors most treasure are as rare as they are striking. Collectors who want a sundial, junonia, nutmeg, Scotch bonnet, lion's paw, or some other scarce native shell may have to buy it from one of the many Sanibel and Captiva shell shops. The shops purchase rare shells from professional shell hunters, commercial fishermen, and shrimp boat captains, whose nets may dredge up deep-water shells.

Sanibel shell shops are stocked with exotic and native shells, and they sell more of the exotics. Suzy Johnson, who owns a shop, says that fewer than 25 percent of her customers ask for shells native to Sanibel. Some buyers naively assume that all shells in Sanibel and Captiva shops are home-grown. The average buyer isn't concerned about the shell's origins; that person just wants a souvenir shell. Whether or not it was plucked from the *Costa de Carocles* doesn't seem to matter.

Actually, Sanibel's long association with shells has a cosmopolitan bent. The town held its first community shell fair in 1927. Only native shells were shown then, but the fair soon became a showplace for shells from all over the world. Today the fair is a major scientific and artistic attraction, held each year at the Sanibel Community Center during the first week in March.

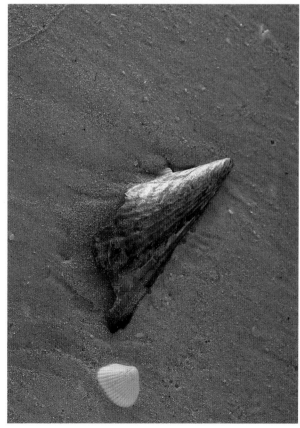

Above: The Florida horse conch (Pleuroploca gigantea) grows up to nineteen inches long, the largest of the state's marine snails and one of the largest univalve snails, or gastropods, in the world. It preys mainly on relatives, such as tulip snails and lightning whelks. It is still fairly common in the muddy sand of Sanibel bays, but small specimens predominate. ***Right:*** Fragments of stiff pen shells (Atrina rigida) are common in the wrack of Sanibel and Captiva beaches. One of the most common of the island shells, the pen has a silky pearl-and-blue iridescence that makes it one of the islands' most striking shells, too.

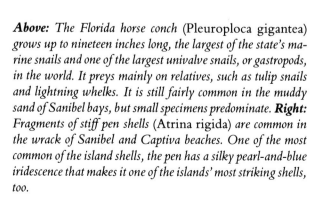

75

Although not indigenous to Sanibel, or Florida, periwinkles (Vinca rosea) have escaped from gardens and become established throughout open areas on the island, including the J.N. "Ding" Darling National Wildlife Refuge. One of Sanibel's main thoroughfares, Periwinkle Way, may have been named for these bright, sprightly flowers, or it may have been named for the seashell by the same name.

THE "DING" DARLING REFUGE

Sanibel's privately owned, undeveloped lands may not always be. But as Bird Westall says, "We'll always have the refuge." On Sanibel "the refuge" is the J.N. "Ding" Darling National Wildlife Refuge, owned and administered by the U.S. Fish and Wildlife Service, the same people who have about 430 units in the refuge system throughout the United States.

The refuge is invaluable to Sanibel. Some of it is submerged land, but the refuge still accounts for about 40 percent of Sanibel's acreage. The entire refuge encompasses 5,030 acres, of which 4,728 are in the main tract on Sanibel's bay side. The Bailey tract is a one hundred-acre site on Tarpon Bay Road. The refuge also includes the gulf front, three-acre Perry tract, seven-acre Runyon Key, and one hundred ninety acres on Buck Key.

The main refuge tract is a sprawling patchwork of mangrove, upland, canals, inlets, bays, and hidden Calusa mounds. Nearly twenty-eight hundred acres of the tract is a designated wilderness of mangrove swamp forest and water. Visitors don't hike through the Darling wilderness; they ride alligators. Or they rent canoes at the Tarpon Bay refuge concession and paddle the marked three-mile Commodore Creek Trail. The refuge also has a marked canoe trail on Buck Key.

Visitors who drive the one-way, five-mile Wildlife Drive through the main refuge see bays, channels, mangrove forest, and birds at every turn. People who walk or bicycle the road, or park their cars and set out on a side trail, see and

hear more of the refuge's creatures. A short boardwalk leads visitors into a red mangrove swamp. The four-mile Indigo Trail travels through woodlands near the visitor center and eventually along an earthen dike through a mangrove swamp by the observation tower on Wildlife Drive. The fifteen hundred-foot Shell Mound Trail heads from Wildlife Drive into a dark jungle of West Indian plants edged by mangroves. The attraction there is a Calusa shell mound overgrown with tangled greenery.

Many tourists roll through the refuge like tumbleweeds, never stopping for more than a glance. It is true that sometimes there isn't much wildlife to see from the road. The driver who chooses to enter the refuge at midday, especially if the tide is up, won't see anywhere near the birdlife that the driver at dawn or dusk will see. A visit at anytime is enhanced by low tide. Departing tides bare the mudflats for ibis, egrets, herons, roseate spoonbills, and shorebirds.

In recent years the auto traffic in the refuge has intensified to an average of about five hundred cars per day. The increase in human use — an estimated 800,000 people visit the refuge in a year — has already prompted some changes. The visitor center was built in 1982. More recently, a modest entrance fee was imposed, and a gate, photosensitized not to open before dawn, was installed. No one sees the refuge sky and water in predawn pink anymore. A growing concern of the Fish and Wildlife Service is whether a rising tide of auto

Seen from the air, Wildlife Drive snakes through the mangrove swamps and bays of the J.N. "Ding" Darling National Wildlife Refuge. The refuge was established in 1945 as the Sanibel Island National Wildlife Refuge. In 1967, it was renamed to honor Darling, the man who was instrumental in its preservation.

J.N. "Ding" Darling once lived in this house-on-stilts in the Roosevelt Channel, a narrow passage of salt water between Captiva Island and Buck Key, a stone's throw away.

The Commodore Creek canoe trail winds for one and one-half miles through a green jungle of mangroves in the refuge. Another refuge canoe trail offers a four-mile trek through the mangrove fringe of Buck Key.

traffic and bird observation is compatible with the best interests of the birds.

The earthen-dike road through today's refuge was completed in the early 1960s when the land was held by the state and private owners. The dike was engineered by Tom Wood, the manager of the refuge at that time; Wayne Miller of Lee County Mosquito Control District; and Colon Moore, who performed most of the labor and earned the sobriquet "Virtuoso of the Dragline."

The dike's main purpose was to curb the mosquito population. In the late 1950s, the county had begun to attack the legions of Sanibel mosquitoes with a system of canals, impoundments, and water-control structures. When they had dealt with one part of the island, the mosquito control lads looked for another. Charles LeBuff recalls that in those days, the Mosquito Control District pretty much dug and diked as it pleased.

The plan that Wood and Miller hatched for what eventually became Wildlife Drive was to build a dike by dredging soil and leveling the top

of it for a road. The dike and a series of canals would flood low areas and eliminate the mud flats where the mosquitoes bred. The higher areas would be dried out, eliminating them as breeding sites. The waterways and new impoundments would allow mosquito-eating fish permanent access to mosquito populations that survived. The roadway was encouraged by the newly formed J.N. "Ding" Darling Memorial Committee, the members of which foresaw it as a means of shuttling people comfortably into the island's fascinating mangrove community.

Mosquitos were very much on the minds of Sanibel residents and visitors in the 1950s. A single trap hung by the Sanibel ferry landing in September 1950 caught almost three hundred sixty-six thousand mosquitoes—in one night. Dr. Maurice Provost, an entomologist with the Florida Board of Health, computed the density of salt-marsh mosquito eggs in the Sanibel Slough to be as high as two billion per acre in 1951. "One had to see Pat Murphy going around his Jeep mail

Overleaf: *A silhouette in sunset gold, a black-necked stilt* (Himantopus mexicanus) *stalks across a pond in the refuge's Bailey tract. Adjacent to Tarpon Bay Road, the Bailey tract is one of several segments that compose the five thousand acre J.N. "Ding" Darling National Wildlife Refuge.*

delivery route in July wrapped in Eskimo clothing and netting . . . to appreciate these infamous Sanibel mosquitoes," Dr. Provost wrote in the *Florida Naturalist.*

The refuge was named for Jay Norwood Darling, also known as "Ding." He was a man of exceptional talent and achievement. Said an aquaintance: " 'Ding' knew what was desirable and what was possible, and he had a genius for their productive compromise."

Darling was, among other things, a syndicated political cartoonist for the *Des Moines Register.* His cartoons, which often showed a strong proconservation bias, earned two Pulitzer Prizes. By the time Darling made his first trip to Captiva in 1936, his work had already caught the eye of President Franklin D. Roosevelt, and he had been appointed director of the U.S. Bureau of Biological Survey, later the U.S. Fish and Wildlife Service. Darling at various times was a leader of the Izaak Walton League, a founder of the National Wildlife Federation, and a member of the National Audubon Society Board of Directors. In 1934 he initiated the federal duck stamp program, which is still a major source of revenue for wetlands acquisition.

Darling once owned a tiny cottage at the end of a dock on Captiva, and for some twenty-five years he was active and influential in conservation issues that affected the islands. He was instrumental in having the Sanibel National Wildlife Refuge established in 1945 and in the purchase of the Bailey tract in 1954.

"Ding" Darling died in 1962 at the age of 86. The J.N. "Ding" Darling Memorial Committee was created in the same year. The committee was influential in having the Sanibel Island National Wildlife Refuge renamed for Ding in 1967. One mission accomplished, the committee evolved into the Sanibel-Captiva Conservation Foundation, now the islands' foremost local conservation organization.

Today the refuge is one of the most popular in the nationwide chain, and it has been a fine steward of the land. The refuge protects habitat and wildlife, provides wildlife and habitat interpretation, and manages the habitat for wildlife through water control, eradication of exotic plants, and controlled burns. The refuge also remembers the man who left his signature on Sanibel and Captiva as well as on hundreds of cartoons.

Mangroves crowd the Shell Mound Trail, which loops from Wildlife Drive around a Calusa shell mound. The mound itself is overgrown by a jungle of cacti and West Indian vegetation.

ISLANDS OF SEA
AND SKY

From sea level, on a bright day, the island region from Charlotte Harbor south into San Carlos Bay is a scape of color: clumps and borders of dark, green-daubed mangroves, blue sky, and aquamarine water. On a week day in the autumn, a day made for fishing, you can anchor somewhere between mangrove clumps and have the place to yourself. The ospreys and eagles won't bother you if you don't swim like a fish. The pelicans will leave you alone, too, but watch your bait. Noise? Only the wind strumming on your line and, with any luck at all, the scream of your drag being tested by a bull redfish big enough to scare you.

This is the kind of company that Sanibel keeps, an expanse of sea and sky and neighboring islands that either rim or are in Charlotte Harbor, Pine Island Sound, and San Carlos Bay. Some are barrier islands, but most of them lie in quiet bay waters, protected by the outlying group. Many of these are mere islets, framed in a tangle of mangrove roots and muck. A few are privately owned. A few more, popular with colonial birds, are owned by the U.S. Fish and Wildlife Service and administered from Sanibel.

This neighborhood shares an astonishing biological richness because of its estuarine nature. Charlotte Harbor is the confluence of the Myakka and Peace rivers, and the Caloosahatchee River flows into San Carlos Bay. Within a distance of about twenty miles, from Gasparilla Island south to lower Sanibel, is a delightfully bewildering

world of marine and terrestrial life.

The blending of saltwater and freshwater in an estuary, the meeting place of river and sea, is extremely important in the life cycles of many marine species such as juvenile shrimp, snook, sea trout, and redfish. Their lives are governed by the need for nutrients and the fluctuating levels of water salinity they find in estuaries. Estuarine salinity changes with tides, location within the estuarine zone, and the seasonal cycles of rain and drought.

Sanibel's closest neighbor in the island region is Captiva, separated from Sanibel only by Blind Pass, an ocean thread. Geographically and geologically, Sanibel and Captiva are sisters. Someone who had visited neither might suspect they were identical twins, given the fundamental equality of hyphenated words, to wit: Sanibel-Captiva Chamber of Commerce, Sanibel-Captiva Conservation Foundation, Sanibel-Captiva Audubon Society, and so on. In fact, Captiva is a wisp of island, about one-twentieth the size of Sanibel and not quite five miles in length. On the lower end of Captiva, Sanibel-Captiva Road walks a tightrope to avoid the gulf on one side and the narrow channel between Captiva and Buck Key on the other.

Captiva is almost entirely developed. It is an island of secluded old wealth with comfortable shorefront homes hidden by dense thickets of coconut palm, sea grape, Australian pine, hibiscus, and other subtropical plants. It is also an is-

Roseate spoonbills gather near the observation tower in the J.N. "Ding" Darling National Wildlife Refuge. Low evening tides lure scores of the spoonbills to the food-rich tidal flats.

The mangrove-edged islands of Charlotte Harbor and San Carlos Bay are prime habitats for wading birds. The black-crowned night heron (Nycticorax nycticorax) is one of the most retiring of the waders, generally feeding at night and fleeing from human approach. With several waders in decline, Florida has identified the black-crowned heron as a "species of special concern."

land of restaurants, shops, and a few resorts. The northern third of Captiva is owned by a single resort, South Seas Plantation.

Unlike Sanibel, Captiva is not incorporated. It depends heavily on Lee County, the island's administrator, for erosion funds and equipment. A visitor's impression is that Captiva's southern tip would naturally erode away without the county's efforts to restore the beach by pumping sand up from the gulf.

The hurricane of 1921 cut Redfish Pass through Captiva, leaving the "new" Upper Captiva Island. Long-time Captiva resident Joe Wightman once remembered that the inlet earned its name in 1923 when the water ran red with great schools of coppery redfish. Fishermen still frequent Upper Captiva along with shellers. This island is slowly being developed, although it has no bridges either to Captiva or the mainland.

Cayo Costa Island, at the mouth of Charlotte Harbor, is a favorite of outdoor enthusiasts. Hikers, shellers, boaters, anglers and campers love the island's woods, beaches, and deep, restless waters.

Cayo lies on a north-south axis north of Upper Captiva and separated from it by Captiva Pass. Together, Cayo Costa, the Captivas, and Sanibel form a broken chain of gulf-front barrier islands shaped like a hockey stick, Sanibel being the blade.

Ninety percent of Cayo Costa's twenty-two hundred acres compose Cayo Costa State Preserve. Undeveloped and heavily wooded, the preserve is isolated from the mainland. It has rustic, seaside cabins and primitive camping. Fishing and shellfishing around Cayo Costa can be exceptional, but swimming is treacherous because of fast currents and sharp dropoffs in many places.

Across the deep water of Boca Grande Pass, at the north end of Cayo Costa, are Gasparilla Island and the town of Boca Grande, accessible by road from Placida. The northernmost of the Charlotte Harbor barrier islands, Gasparilla is known for its deep harbor, manicured estates, and its claim as the world's tarpon fishing capital.

Gasparilla Island enjoyed fleeting prosperity in the early 1900s with the advent of rail service, the

Striped mullet (Mugil cephalus) *are an important part of the marine food web in southwest Florida. Mullet are acrobatic, but they decline bait and confound sport fishermen. Cast nets are used to take mullet, and smoked mullet is a regional delicacy.*

A royal tern (Sterna maxima) *passes overhead as a brown pelican* (Pelecanus occidentalis) *dives toward the sea and a school of fish. White pelicans* (Pelecanus erythrorhynchos) *are also found among the islands, especially during winter. White pelicans fish by swimming in loose convoys and using their huge gular pouches as dip nets.*

Brown pelicans and other water birds build nests on several mangrove islets in Charlotte Harbor and San Carlos Bay. The region is one of the brown pelican's strongholds. Since not all brown pelicans nest simultaneously, the nesting season, from courtship through the rearing of young, may last from January into late summer in southwest Florida.

establishment of a phosphate shipping operation, and the arrival of numerous wealthy tourists, some of whom built island estates. After a period of decline and slumber, the island is booming again with pricey residential development along its gulf shores and an influx of sightseers and anglers.

In the upper regions of Pine Island Sound, on the backside of Cayo Costa, are Cabbage Key and Useppa Island. They are neighbors without much in common. Cabbage Key, at channel marker sixty in the Intracoastal Waterway, is essentially a Calusa shell midden fringed with mangroves and capped by a house-turned-inn. Originally built by novelist Mary Roberts Rinehart in 1938, the inn has six rooms for rent, a bar, restaurant, and one-of-a-kind decor—approximately twenty-five thousand autographed dollar bills covering the walls and ceiling. The custom of leaving a greenback began, the story goes, when a fisherman en route to the high seas left a buck to reserve his cold brew.

Useppa sits directly across the Intracoastal Waterway from its rustic neighbor. Useppa is a private refuge for high rollers, wealthy boaters, and fishermen who could chum for tarpon, the silver kings, with silver dollars. It's also home for several ospreys who may be the only freeloaders on the island. Like Cayo Costa and Gasparilla, Useppa is handy to the superb tarpon fishing each May through August in Boca Grande Pass and in nearby waters.

East of the Pine Island Sound barrier islands is Pine Island, easily the largest in this neighborhood of islands. The undeveloped interior of Pine Island is forested with native pines. Much of its perimeter is sheltered by mangroves; the island is surrounded by bay waters—Pine Island Sound, Charlotte Harbor, Matlacha Pass, and San Carlos Bay.

Without the lure of a gulf-front beach, Pine Island languished until recently. It was a relatively undisturbed patch of modest homes, cottages, fish shacks, woods, and mangroves. It was a favorite hangout of sport, commercial, and shell fishermen. With the rapid development of the Lee County mainland, Pine Island is being swept by rapid growth also, and its repute as a getaway for fishing may fade.

And development, with all of its tentacles, is the future that all of these islands will have to confront. Even a state preserve like Cayo Costa will be affected by what happens on the lands and in the waters around it. No island, these days, is an island unto itself.

The endangered wood stork (Mycteria americana), the only North American stork, can still be found in the island wetlands. The wood stork depends on precise water levels so that it can catch sufficient numbers of fish for its young. The stork population has plummeted in recent years as manipulation of water levels and drought in south Florida has often created too high or too low water levels.

MAINTAINING THE CIVILIZED WILDERNESS

If you compare the Sanibel of today with the Sanibel of 20 years ago, it's been destroyed. If you compare Sanibel to the rest of Florida, it's a paradise.

— Mark "Bird" Westall
Sanibel Councilman, 1990

If, as Westall contends, part of the paradise is lost, the important thing is that part of it isn't. A central problem in the future, then, is how to retain what is left in the face of increasing development and tourism. Westall further suggests that the restoration of the paradise lost is also a problem to be addressed.

A buzz word on Sanibel is "island character." Whatever it means— "different things to different people," Westall says—island character and its preservation are on the minds of many Sanibel residents. To Westall and many conservationist allies, the character of Sanibel Island is inextricably wed to the fundamental idea that, at least on this island, humans should, and do, coexist with the natural environment, rendering as little disruption to that environment as possible.

Certainly the island has a proud tradition of concern for the environment. Part of that tradition has been to oppose outside forces that would have compromised the Sanibel environment. Opposition culminated in incorporation. As Charles LeBuff, a former councilman says, "Incorporation saved Sanibel." Ever since the early days when Thomas Edison and Teddy Roosevelt visited, Sanibel's natural beauty has been her si-

ren. But there are always those who would enjoy the fruits of the island's natural character without comprehending what they really are or how difficult they are to maintain. There are residents on Sanibel who love wildlife—as long as the wildlife stays on the refuge. "One lady's idea of coexistence with wildlife," says Westall, "meant that wildlife needed a permit to come visit her."

There are some disquieting murmurs on the island. "In the old days we had a higher number of staunch environmentalists," says Westall. "Now we're a real community with more people with old ways of thinking from up north. Many talk environmentalism but paying for it is something else." Rising taxes and changing residents are unavoidable. As newcomers swell the island population and threaten to dilute the conservation ethic that is the backbone of island character, Westall observes, "We need to do a better job of educating the public. It's a tough job to make people understand what living on Sanibel means."

Maintaining total harmony in Sanibel's civilized wilderness will never be simple. Consider the spoonbill that reposes, nicely mounted, in the glassed habitat display case of the refuge visitor center. Most spoonbills come to the refuge by design; this one came by accident. The bird apparently had been feeding in a marsh on a Sanibel golf course. A golfer, presumably determined to card a birdy, struck a drive that brained the spoonbill. But that is the nature of civilized wilderness; wild animals will, from time to time, leave their pro-

A snowy egret (Egrette thula), *plumes erect after being agitated by another snowy, symbolizes the wilderness appeal of Sanibel Island. Thousands of birds find refuge in the uplands and wetlands of the island.*

91

Left: Wildflowers grow throughout the year on subtropical Sanibel Island. The coral bean (Erythrina herbacea) *was photographed in March.* **Below:** *Shorebirds congregate on Sanibel beaches, especially during spring and fall migrations. Controlled development has helped maintain beach habitat for these sanderlings* (Calidris alba) *and their kin.*

tected environment and wander into an altered environment that may be hazardous to their existence.

More important than the occasional conflicts between humans and animals is the environment as a whole. Will the island's natural systems, such as the interior wetlands, be maintained and, when necessary, restored? Sometimes the status flow isn't sufficient.

For all of its flaws, the Sanibel concept of coexistence with wildlife and the natural environment has been a noble and largely successful undertaking. An enormous, grassroots feeling of sensitivity toward and appreciation for the environment pervades this community. It is reflected in the pictures and posters displayed in shops and hotel lobbies. It is reflected in the good works of volunteers who care for injured animals at the CROW (Care and Rehabilitation of Wildlife) center and maintain saltwater aquaria in the Sanibel Elementary School. The sensitivity is reflected, too, in the environmental organizations that call Sanibel home, including the Sanibel-Captiva Conservation Foundation, which owns and protects over one thousand acres of ecologically important land on Sanibel, Upper Captiva, and Buck Key; the "Ding" Darling Wildlife Society, which works cooperatively with the U.S. Fish and Wildlife Service in wildlife interpretation and education; the Sanibel-Captiva Audubon Society; the Sanibel-Captiva Shell Club; the International Osprey Foundation; Caretta Research; CROW; the Tarpon Bay Research Laboratory, a cooperative venture of the Fish and Wildlife Service and other groups; and the city of Sanibel's Wildlife Committee, established to inspect future development sites and, whenever possible, resettle animals elsewhere.

This sensitivity toward the environment is not only good for Sanibel, but for the people who come here for just a day or a week or a month. People can learn a great deal here about environmental stewardship and ecological systems. Some of them undoubtedly take their lessons home and apply them elsewhere.

The ultimate future of Sanibel, of course, will not be determined solely by the wisdom of local men and women who strive to keep Sanibel a cut above. Growing populations on Pine Island and on the Florida mainland will affect the health of Sanibel waters and wildlife. The burgeoning mainland populace means greater day-use of Sanibel, where facilities are already stretched to capacity during the season.

Meanwhile, as Sanibel confronts the future, the island fairly shimmers as an example of how humans can coexist with the natural environment and reject a destructive way of life. In a state where the excesses of development have shattered coastal ecosystems in many quarters, Sanibel Island is, in the island vernacular, a junonia.

INDEXED LIST OF SANIBEL'S NATURAL HISTORY

This is a partial list of the plant and animal species, natural history, human history, and recreation found on Sanibel Island, with page number references. Use this list to acquaint yourself with what you have found, or will find, on Sanibel and Captiva islands. The symbol *(p)* indicates that a photo of the plant or animal is found on the page.

ABOUT THE AUTHOR

Author with bluefish. (Photo by Melvin Stone)

During his college and early teaching years, Lynn Stone worked as a part-time sports writer in Connecticut and Illinois. He then taught English for several years in Illinois and Florida. Now he is the author of more than sixty books for children and young adults on natural history topics.

Lynn is a freelance writer and natural history photographer. Not only does he spend two months each year photographing wildlife in Florida, he also travels the world—North America, Europe, Australia, and Africa—with his cameras, taking nature shots. His photos have appeared in *Time, National Wildlife, International Wildlife,* and on Sierra Club and Audubon calendars, as well as in many other publications.

Since 1967 Lynn has been a regular visitor to Sanibel, and he lived in Sarasota, Florida, for two years. He has written articles about Florida's natural history for *Florida Wildlife, Florida Sportsman, Learning, Islands, Oceans,* and *Animal Kingdom.* His article topics include loggerheads, mangroves, sea grass ecology, Sanibel Island, the Florida bog frog, and various state parks.

Lynn Stone says that his earliest memories center around his interest in wildlife. He still enjoys all aspects of the outdoors, including fishing, canoeing, snorkeling, pheasant hunting, hiking, and especially, wildlife photography.

In the late afternoon, a brown pelican duels wave crests in the Gulf of Mexico after a shallow dive for baitfish.